The Pitman Motor-cyclists' Library

The Book of the
BSA BANTAM

Covering the Practical Maintenance of all
1948–1970 BSA Bantam Two-stroke
Motor-cycles

W. C. Haycraft, F.R.S.A.

Revised by
A. G. Lupton, C.Eng, M.I.Mech.E.

Pitman Publishing

Sixth edition 1972
Reprinted 1973

SIR ISAAC PITMAN AND SONS LTD.
Pitman House, Parker Street, Kingsway, London WC2B 5PB
P.O. Box 46038, Portal Street, Nairobi, Kenya

SIR ISAAC PITMAN (AUST.) PTY. LTD.
Pitman House, 158 Bouverie Street, Carlton, Victoria 3053, Australia

PITMAN PUBLISHING COMPANY S.A. LTD.
P.O. Box 11231, Johannesburg, South Africa

PITMAN PUBLISHING CORPORATION
6 East 43rd Street, New York, N.Y. 10017, U.S.A.

SIR ISAAC PITMAN (CANADA) LTD.
495 Wellington Street West, Toronto 135, Canada

THE COPP CLARK PUBLISHING COMPANY
517 Wellington Street West, Toronto 135, Canada

ISBN: 0 273 36176 7

Text set in 8/9 pt. Monotype Times New Roman, printed by
photolithography, and bound in Great Britain at The Pitman Press, Bath
G3—(G.4419:19)

Preface

The two-stroke B.S.A. Bantam was introduced to the British public at the 1948 Motor Cycle Show. Since its introduction it has "caught on" in a truly remarkable manner. This is perhaps not surprising considering the Bantam's alluring looks, lightness (Model D7: 214 lb), and satisfying all-round performance.

The Bantam steers with precision, holds the road tenaciously and can cruise at around 40 m.p.h. almost indefinitely without "fuss." Fuel consumption is *extremely* low. As in the case of other renowned B.S.A. models, easy starting and thorough reliability are predominant characteristics.

With every motor-cycle, thorough reliability over a prolonged period depends, ultimately, on how the machine is maintained by its owner. The purpose of this handbook is to provide in a convenient and digestible form all essential instructions necessary for the efficient maintenance of *all* 1948–70 *Bantams*, so as to assist owners to obtain the maximum pleasure and mileage per gallon and per hour.

Note that instructions are included in this book for competition as well as touring models, and that all instructions for Model D7 apply also to the 1965–6 de luxe Model D7D/L which is almost identical. In August 1966 the Model 7 was replaced by a more powerful version known as the D10 (fitted with either a three or four-speed gearbox), which in turn was superseded for the 1968 season by the D14/4 (still more powerful, and incorporating the four-speed gearbox). In 1970 this model became known simply as the Bantam 175.

In conclusion I sincerely thank B.S.A. Motor Cycles Ltd. of Birmingham, 11, for valuable assistance in regard to technical data, and for according me permission to reproduce some B.S.A. copyright illustrations. I also thank Wico-Pacy Group Sales Ltd., Amal Ltd., and other firms for their helpful co-operation.

W. C. HAYCRAFT

Contents

1 Handling a Bantam

It is assumed that you are about to purchase or have just taken delivery of a new or second-hand 123 cm³ or 174 cm³ B.S.A. Bantam, a machine of which you will doubtless be proud and find easy to handle, even if you have had no previous experience.

Should you yourself be a complete novice, obtain, read, and thoroughly digest the *Highway code*. A full knowledge of this booklet is essential to ensure safe riding and compliance with the law. See that you have a crash helmet for use on long and short runs. Accident statistics show that motorcyclists are particularly prone to serious head injuries. Such injuries can have disastrous effects.

Various Preliminaries. Before you can legally ride a Bantam on the public highway you must comply with various essential preliminaries. In this book which is primarily concerned with Bantam maintenance it is only possible to deal with these preliminaries in the barest outline.

If you purchase a new or second-hand Bantam from a reputable dealer, you will almost invariably find him ready to assist you with most of the essential preliminaries (licensing, number plates, insurance, etc.), and it may only be necessary for you to settle financially with the dealer, either cash down or on hire-purchase terms, and then take personal delivery of your Bantam or have it delivered by the dealer to your address.

As regards the essential preliminaries, here is a brief outline of them. You must:

1. Insure against all third-party risks (injuries to persons other than yourself or a pillion passenger, if carried). If you purchase your machine on hire-purchase terms, the dealer concerned will insist on your taking out a full comprehensive insurance, which is always advisable in the case of a valuable new machine.

2. Obtain a "Certificate of Insurance" or a cover note (for a new machine) pending the issue of a certificate by your insurance company. Without either, you will be unable to obtain a registration licence.

3. Obtain a registration licence and registration book[1] (Form V.E. 1/2),

---

[1] On Form V.E. 1/2 you are required to state the engine and frame numbers. On 1948–52 Bantams the engine number is located at the front of the crankcase on the near side, between the engine fixing lugs. On 1953–70 models the engine number is on top of the crankcase, below the cylinder. On all 1948–70 Bantams the frame number is located on the bottom of the front down-tube (or at the top of the steering-head tube).

or renew the existing licence (Form V.E.1/A) if expired. All B.S.A. 123 cm³, 148 cm³ and 174 cm³ Bantams are taxed at the rate of £5 per annum. If a sidecar is attached (not advised), no additional tax is necessary.

4. Fit the registration licence disc in the waterproof licence holder on the near side of the front forks.

5. See that the index letters and registration numbers allocated to your Bantam are painted correctly on the number plates.

Fig. 1. Cheap to run, easy to maintain, light and thoroughly reliable—the attractive 1968 174 cm³ Bantam (Model D14/4)

This popular general-purpose mount weighing only 214 lb has a de luxe finish in electric blue and black with chromium plated tank panels. The other 1968 B.S.A. lightweight, the 174 cm³ "Bantam Sports" (Model D14/45) is basically similar. Both these modern machines have a highly efficient two-stroke engine with built-in gearbox, a quickly detachable light-alloy cylinder head, petroil lubrication, coil ignition, battery lighting, a most comfortable dualseat, telescopic front forks, and swinging arm rear suspension

6. Mount "L" plates at the front and rear if you are a "learner."

7. Obtain a "Provisional" (six months) or "Qualified" (three-year) driving licence (Form D.L.1.), whichever is appropriate. You are *not* entitled to a full licence for Group G unless you are aged *sixteen* and have complied with one of these conditions:

(*a*) You have held a licence (other than a provisional or Visitor's licence), authorizing the driving of vehicles of the class or description applied for, within a period of ten years ending on the date of coming into force of the licence applied for.

(*b*) You have passed the prescribed driving test (a test passed when serving in H.M. Forces is valid) during the above period.

8. If you carry a pillion passenger while a "learner," see that he or she sits *astride* a proper pillion seat or dualseat securely *fixed* to the machine, and has a "qualified" driving licence.

9. Verify that the fork-mounted or headlamp-mounted speedometer *is* in proper working order. A Smith's speedometer (driven from the rear wheel) is fitted as standard. To comply with the law the speedometer must indicate within ±10 per cent accuracy when 30 m.p.h. is being exceeded, and be illuminated at night.

10. If the machine is second-hand, make sure it is thoroughly roadworthy. Check that *both* brakes are in proper working order, that the front and rear lights are functioning correctly (with *rear* number plate illuminated) and that the horn gives "audible warning of approach." A bulb horn is fitted to a.c. models, but an electric horn is available as an extra for 1951–65 Bantams with Wipac a.c. direct lighting, and is standard equipment on models having a Lucas or Wipac battery-lighting set.

11. If you own a Bantam registered for the first time after 1st July, 1953, you must use an "ignition-suppression" type sparking plug which does not interfere with radio and television sets.

12. If you are a "learner" and feel qualified to take a driving test, apply for one on Form D.L.26.

13. If your B.S.A. Bantam was first registered more than three years ago, obtain an MoT certificate (see page 15).

Vetting a Second-hand Bantam. Make sure that all accessories and equipment are securely mounted. With the appropriate spanners check over the external nuts for tightness, paying special attention to the wheel-spindle nuts and the external nuts on the engine and those securing it to the frame. See that there is no excessive "shake" in the wheel and steering-head bearings, that the saddle or dualseat is comfortable, that the rear chain and wheel sprocket are not badly worn, and that the tyres are in reasonably good condition. Above all, make sure that no excessive mechanical noise emanates from the engine when it is turned over or started up. Nothing should be taken for granted where a second-hand machine is concerned, though many examples (especially where there has been only one previous owner) are in first-rate condition and require little or no attention before taking the road (*see also* paragraph 10 above).

Handlebars Adjustable for Angle. Should the riding position not be the best obtainable, having regard to your own particular physique, you can vary the angle of the handlebars to some extent by loosening the four bolts on the top of the handlebar clamps and then turning the bars to the desired angle. On the 1954 Model D3 and many D3 and D5 models, slacken the four nuts clamping the handlebar bend to the aluminium cover. The nuts are situated below the bars, two in front and two at the rear. Having done this, you can then turn the bars to the required angle, Be sure that you afterwards retighten the bolts or nuts securely. On competition models the footrests are adjustable to six different positions. To adjust the angle of each footrest, first remove its securing nut and lightly tap the footrest off its hexagonal shaft. Then replace the footrest in the required position and tighten its securing nut.

THE BANTAM CONTROLS

If you have never before handled a Bantam, you should get quite familiar with the control layout before making any attempt to start up. Note the exact location of each control and consider what it is for and how it is operated. Also reflect on which controls are used in conjuction with each other. It is a sound idea to sit astride the saddle and twiddle the various controls while imagining what the effect would be were the engine running.

Three Control Groups. The Bantam controls (*see* Figs. 3–5) are mostly located on the handlebars, and for convenience may be divided into three groups: (1) engine controls, (2) motor-cycle controls, and (3) electrical controls.

1. The engine controls comprise: (*a*) the throttle twist-grip, (*b*) the carburettor strangler or (on 1966–70 models) the air control, (*c*) the ignition switch, on models with coil ignition, (*d*) the decompressor on competition models only, and (*e*) the kick-starter.

2. The motor-cycle controls are: (*a*) the clutch lever, (*b*) the foot gear-change pedal, (*c*) the front brake lever, and (*d*) the rear brake pedal.

3. The electrical controls are: (*a*) the lighting switch, (*b*) the dipper switch, and (*c*) the horn button.

The Throttle Twist-grip. This is mounted on the handlebar extremity on the right side. Turning the rubber-covered grip *inwards* (i.e. towards the rider) raises the throttle slide in the single-lever needle-jet Amal carburettor and admits more mixture, thus increasing engine speed. Turning the grip outwards closes the throttle and decreases engine speed. Full movement: about $\frac{1}{4}$ turn.

The Carburettor Strangler (1949–65 Models). No air lever is provided on the handlebars. Instead a strangler is embodied in the bell of the carburettor air-intake and controls the amount of air admitted to the carburettor. The strangler consists of a perforated plate the rotation of which masks or unmasks similar bell perforations.

Except when starting from cold, when the strangler should be *momentarily* closed (*see* page 12), the strangler should at all times be kept fully open. To close the strangler in order to provide a very rich mixture, *raise* the small lever on the right side of the carburettor.

The Carburettor Air Control (1966 Models). A shutter is not provided on the bell of the carburettor air-intake. Instead a carburettor air slide is included, and this is controlled by a spring-loaded plunger on top of the Amal instrument as shown in Fig. 2.

To close the air control in order to reduce the amount of air sucked into the carburettor and thereby enrich the air–petrol mixture, press down the plunger as far as possible and then rotate it until it is secured by the locking

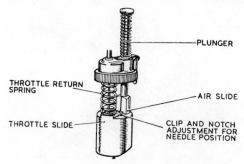

Fig. 2. Showing the air-control plunger and air slide fitted to the Amal "Monobloc" carburettor on all 1966 models

Depress the plunger only momentarily when difficulty is experienced in starting a cold engine

clip. Closing this control is recommended *if necessary* when starting up a *cold* engine. Immediately the engine fires, open it to obtain the normal air supply by further rotating the spring-loaded plunger until it is released from the locking clip.

Never ride with the air control closed and when using the control for starting, close it for a *brief* period only.

The Carburettor Air Control (1967–70 Models). An air slide is included in the specification of the Amal "Concentric" carburettor fitted to these models (*see* Fig. 16) and is controlled by a lever on the right handlebar. To close the air slide for cold starting purposes only, turn the lever in an anti-clockwise direction (away from the rider), but at all other times the lever should be kept in the fully clockwise position.

Special Note on Carburettors for All Models. It must be emphasized that excessive use of the strangler or air control, as the case may be, is likely to cause liquid petrol to enter the crankcase and render starting almost impossible until the petrol is drained off by removing the smaller of the two drain plugs beneath the crankcase.

The Ignition Switch (1950–3 Models). On Bantams equipped with Lucas coil-ignition and battery-lighting equipment, an ignition key is provided in the centre of the headlamp lighting switch. This does *not* apply to 1954–66 models with Wipac rectifier and battery lighting. The Lucas ignition key has three positions:

EMG—Emergency position for starting when the battery is fully discharged and it is necessary to switch the generator output direct into the ignition circuit by disconnecting the battery.

Fig. 3. The Model D1, D3 Bantam handlebar controls, speedometer, horn, etc.

Above is a pre-1958 Model D1 with Wico-Pacy flywheel generator and direct lighting. On the battery models an electric horn is fitted, and an ignition key is provided in the centre of the lighting switch (Lucas only). Competition models have a decompressor lever on the near side of the handlebars. A handlebar screen is available as an extra

1. Combined filler cap and oil measure
2. Dipper switch
3. Clutch lever
4. Lighting switch
5. Smiths 55 m.p.h. speedometer
6. Front-brake lever
7. Throttle twist-grip
8. Bulb horn (direct lighting models)

OFF—Ignition switched off. Battery and generator disconnected.

IGN—Ignition switched on. Battery passing L.T. current through the primary circuit (i.e. coil primary-winding and contact-breaker).

For all normal starting and riding, the ignition switch should be kept in the IGN position. Use the EMG position solely for an emergency start when the battery is badly run down. To obtain the maximum generator output, it may be necessary to move the lighting switch to the "pilot" (P) position. As soon as the engine fires, turn the ignition switch over to the IGN position, otherwise the battery will not be on charge. If the battery is completely "flat," you may have to run for a period with the ignition switch in the EMG position, but this period must never be excessive.

When you "cut" a Bantam engine with Lucas coil-ignition, always remember that you must switch off the ignition, otherwise there is a risk of the battery becoming discharged if the contacts of the contact-breaker happen to be closed. If the battery should be removed from the machine make no attempt to start up the engine (*see* note on page 10).

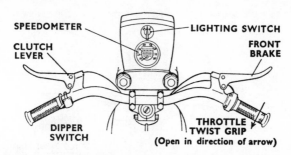

Fig. 4. The Model D5, D7 handlebar controls, lighting switch, etc.
(Wipac direct lighting)
Applicable to 1958–65 Models

The Ignition Switch (1964–70 Models). On 1964–70 coil-ignition models with Wico-Pacy lighting-ignition equipment the ignition switch is separately located from the lighting switch on the offside of the headlamp nacelle. Its three positions are as below.

1. With the switch positioned straight ahead as shown in Fig. 5, the ignition is switched off. When a Bantam is left standing with the engine stopped the ignition should always be left switched off, otherwise after hours (overnight, for example) the battery may become badly discharged through leakage via the contact-breaker, if the contacts happen to be closed.

2. For normal starting procedure the ignition switch should be turned so that position "I" is straight ahead.

3. In the event of the battery being badly discharged for some reason, the ignition switch should be turned until position "E" lies straight ahead; the lighting switch turned to the "OFF" position, and an emergency start attempted. As soon as the engine fires, the ignition switch should be turned to the "I" position. Do not run the engine with the ignition switch in the emergency position for more than 15 minutes.

The Decompressor. On B.S.A. Bantam competition models the first of which was introduced in April, 1949, a decompressor unit (commonly called a compression-release valve) is screwed into the cylinder head and is actuated by a lever on the near side of the handlebars.

The Kick-starter Pedal. This is located on the off-side at the rear end of the engine and gearbox unit, and depressing the pedal turns the engine over. The kick-starter pedal is provided for starting purposes only (with the foot gear-change pedal in "neutral" and the clutch engaged). On Bantam competition models the pedal is of the positive spring-loaded folding type,

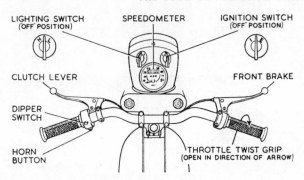

Fig. 5. Handlebar controls for Models D7, D10, D14, and Bantam 175 lighting switch, ignition switch, etc. (Lucas battery lighting)

The above switch arrangement applies to all 1964–70 Bantams with Wipac coil-ignition equipment. The only Lucas component used is the battery. On models D10 and D14 and Bantam 175, the right handlebar also carries the carburettor air control lever (not shown in the illustration) and the headlamp is an independent unit

the pedal automatically remaining in the folded or "action" position, as required.

The Clutch Lever. The handlebar lever for engaging or disengaging the clutch is positioned in front of the left-side handlebar grip. To disengage the clutch (i.e. to disconnect the drive from the engine to the rear wheel), it is necessary to "squeeze" the lever fully. On releasing the lever the clutch automatically becomes re-engaged.

It is necessary to disengage the clutch in order to engage first gear (from "neutral"), with the machine stationary, and when making each subsequent gear change (*see* page 13). No attempt must be made to control the speed of the machine by means of the clutch.

The Foot Gear-change Pedal. On the off-side of the engine and gearbox unit is the toe-operated positive-stop gear-change pedal. This, in conjunction with the clutch (see earlier paragraph), enables "neutral" and the three gear ratios (four on later models) to be obtained as required. It should be particularly noted that the gear-change pedal *always returns to the same position* after each gear change is effected.

To change to a higher gear, it is necessary to *raise* the foot gear-change pedal to its full extent with the toe. Similarly to change to a lower gear, the pedal must be *depressed* with the toe. To obtain first gear from "neutral," a downward movement of the gear-change pedal is required. A gear-change indicator (*see* Fig. 6) is provided on the secondary chain guard on early models.

The Front-brake Lever. This handlebar control lever is similar to the clutch lever, but is mounted on the right side. Observe that the front-brake lever has no connection with the operation of the rear brake, but both brakes should be operated simultaneously to obtain the maximum braking with the minimum wear of the brakes, tyres, and transmission.

The Rear-brake Pedal. Situated on the left side of the machine, this control needs no explaining other than to mention that the brake pedal should be applied progressively and simultaneously with the front-brake lever. Before using either brake, the throttle should always be closed.

The Lighting Switch. On 1948–51 Bantams having direct-lighting equipment, the lighting switch comprises a remote control lever (*see* Fig. 28) on the left side of the handlebars. Moving the switch lever in one direction obtains consecutively the following four positions—OFF, PARK, FULL, and DIP. The park position is intended solely for use when the machine is stationary (the parking bulb being lit by a dry battery behind the reflector). On 1952–65 Bantams with direct lighting equipment, the lighting switch (January, 1952, onwards) is built into the headlamp, and has three positions —OFF, LOW, and HEAD (OFF, L, H). A dry battery (in the headlamp) is retained for the LOW position used for parking, but an essential difference from the earlier equipment is the provision of a dipper switch on the handlebars. On Bantams fitted with Lucas (1950–3) or Wipac (1954–66) battery-lighting as an alternative to the Wipac direct-lighting set, the lighting switch, together with the ammeter, is mounted on top of the headlamp shell and also has three positions—OFF, P, H (Lucas) or OFF, L, H (Wipac). A parking bulb is lit with the switch in the P or L position. A double-filament main bulb is provided, and with the switch in the H position, a dipper switch switches over from the main driving beam to the dipped beam. With Wipac battery lighting, maximum generator output occurs with the lighting switch in the L position. If the battery is discharged, turn to position L.

The Dipper Switch. With the 1952–66 Wipac or the 1950–3 Lucas equipment referred to above, the dipper switch is mounted on the left side of the handlebars behind the clutch lever. It controls the switching from main to dipped beam. On all models with direct lighting it is a separate unit clipped to the handlebars.

On all models (except D3, D1) with battery lighting the dipper switch is combined with a horn button in a single housing adjacent to the handlebar grip.

Note that on 1951–2 models with direct-lighting equipment it is important to operate the dipper switch in a *positive* way from right to left, or vice versa. Be careful not to press the switch upwards or downwards, because this may cause a sharp rise in the voltage due to poor electrical contact, and thus a possible failure of the speedometer and tail lamp bulbs.

The Horn Button. On models having an electric horn instead of a bulb horn built into the steering stem (i.e. on Bantams with battery lighting equipment), the horn button is screwed into the front-brake lever bracket on the right side of the handlebars on Models D1, D3 and D5 but on Models D7, D10, D14, and Bantam 175, is combined with the dipper switch. (*See* Fig. 5.)

STARTING PROCEDURE

Use of Petrol Tap. The petrol (or more correctly "petroil") tap is conveniently located beneath the rear end of the tank. During 1948–66 two different designs of tap have been fitted to Bantams.

On 1948 to late 1951 models the tap fitted has two knobs, one being hexagonal in shape, and the other serrated. To *turn on* this type of tap, push in the *hexagon-shaped knob*. To turn off the tap, push in the serrated knob.

Late 1951 and subsequent Bantams have a button-type tap (*see* Fig. 6). In this instance, to turn on the tap, pull out the button and lock it in position by turning anti-clockwise. To turn off the tap, turn the button clockwise and then push it in. Some models have *two* petrol taps of the button type. Keep one tap closed to maintain a petrol reserve.

Battery Leads Disconnected (Lucas). On 1950–3 Bantams with the Lucas coil-ignition and battery-lighting equipment, it is very important never to attempt to start up the engine with the ignition switch in the IGN or EMG position and the battery disconnected.[1] Failure to observe this precaution will adversely affect the equipment, and if the lamps are switched on with the ignition switch in the IGN position, the bulb filaments will undoubtedly be burned out.

Battery Leads Disconnected (Wipac). Many 1954–64 Bantams have Wipac battery-lighting sets; should it be necessary to run the engine continuously with the Varley battery removed and the battery leads disconnected,[2] the *positive* lead must be connected to an earthed portion of the motor-cycle frame on early 1954 models (see page 77). On late 1954 and 1955–70 Bantams with the "positive earth" system, it is necessary to connect the *negative* lead to the frame. Unless this is done, the rectifier may be damaged. On 1956–70 machines, to avoid the risk of fusing all bulbs and burning out the rectifier, completely disconnect the rectifier at the snap connectors and insulate all leads from each other and from earth.

[1] Note that the battery leads must be reconnected with the battery *positive* terminal earthed. Damage to the rectifier will result from reversal of the battery leads.

[2] See that the battery leads are subsequently reconnected with the correct terminal of the battery earthed. Reversal of the battery leads will damage the rectifier. Do not rev. an engine with battery removed.

To Start Up the Engine. It is assumed that fuel and oil replenishment have been attended to, and that the tyre pressures have been checked and if necessary corrected (*see* page 104). To start up proceed as follows:

1. See that the foot gear-change lever is in the "O" or "neutral" position (between first and second gears), and verify that it *is* in this position by observing (where provided) the gear-change indicator (*see* Fig. 6) or by moving the machine freely backwards or forwards.

2. Turn on the petrol tap (*see* page 10), and if the engine is stone cold, momentarily depress the "tickler" on the float chamber of the carburettor.

Fig. 6. Left-side close-up view showing 1953 engine, clutch adjustment, gear-change indicator, rear-brake pedal, etc.

1. *Button type petrol tap*
2. *Gear-change indicator (positions front to rear: 1, 0, 2, 3)*
3. *Grease nipple for clutch withdrawal mechanism*
4. *Lock-nut for clutch adjusting-pin*
5. *Clutch adjusting-pin*
6. *Rear-brake pedal shaft*

If the engine is fairly warm, no flooding of the carburettor should be necessary. Avoid oscillating the "tickler" rapidly because this is liable to damage the rather vulnerable float.

3. Close the air strangler (if the engine is quite cold) by raising the small lever on the offside of the carburettor. Closing the strangler is rarely necessary when starting up after making a brief halt. If dealing with a *cold* 1966 engine which refuses to start, lower the air slide in the carburettor by depressing the air-control plunger (*see* Fig. 2) on top of the carburettor.

In the case of 1967–70 engines the slide is closed by means of a lever on the right handlebar (see page 5).

4. On a 1950–3 Bantam provided with Lucas coil-ignition and d.c. battery-lighting equipment, turn the ignition switch (*see* page 5) in the centre of the lighting switch to the IGN position (the EMG position if the battery is discharged). On a 1964–70 Bantam provided with Wipac coil-ignition and battery lighting, turn the ignition switch until the position marked "I" (*see* Fig. 5) is straight ahead. Unless this is done it will be quite impossible for the engine to fire. For emergency starting *with a discharged battery*, rotate the switch until position "E" is straight ahead. The lighting switch must be in the "OFF" position.

5. Open the throttle slightly by turning the twist-grip a small amount (about one-eighth to one-quarter of its total movement).

6. Turn the engine over slowly until resistance is felt and then smartly by applying a vigorous sweeping thrust on the starter pedal. The engine should fire at the first or second attempt. On a Competition model the starter pedal can be neatly folded as soon as the engine starts up.

7. Immediately the engine fires, open the air strangler or the air slide, according to model (*see* page 5). If very cold weather prevails, however, it may be necessary to run the engine for a brief period before opening the strangler or air slide. Note that either should normally be used only momentarily (*see* special note on page 5). If an emergency start was made, return the ignition switch to its normal position.

8. Should the engine fail to start up quickly, first verify that the petroil mixture is reaching the float chamber of the carburettor. Watch for petrol drips on depressing the "tickler" on the float-chamber lid. Avoid excessive flooding, however. If the fuel supply is in order, remove the sparking plug and inspect it carefully. If necessary, clean it thoroughly and reset the gap to between 0·018 in. and 0·020 in. (0·020–0·025 in., coil ignition).

HINTS ON RIDING

Even if you are absolutely "green," you will quickly master the handling of the machine on the road. The Bantam, besides being light and easy to man-handle, has excellent road manners, and the gear-change pedal is easy to operate. Confidence born of practice is soon acquired.

Practise moving off, gear changing, and stopping on a quiet road until you feel ready to venture forth upon a major road with normal traffic.

Before attempting to negotiate main road traffic it is essential to get so used to handling the Bantam that the operation of the controls becomes instinctive and your reactions immediate. So long as you have to premeditate what you are about to do, you are a road menace.

To Engage First Gear. It is assumed that the gear-change pedal is still in neutral. Now, to engage first gear, disengage the clutch, and with the toe of the foot *depress* the foot gear-change pedal to its *full* extent. Should it be found that first gear does not engage readily, do not attempt to exert force on the pedal, but rock the machine gently backwards and forwards while maintaining gentle foot pressure on the pedal until first gear is *felt* to engage.

Moving Off. Having engaged first gear, open the throttle slightly to avoid stalling the engine, by gently turning the twist-grip inwards, and gradually engage the clutch. Your Bantam will then move off. As it gathers momentum, progressively open the throttle still farther to maintain a steady increase in the speed of the engine and machine.

Changing Up into Second Gear. When your Bantam attains a road speed of 12–15 m.p.h. (10 m.p.h. on models with four-speed gearboxes), change up into second gear. Disengage the clutch, close the throttle slightly, pause a second, and *raise* the foot gear-change pedal *fully* (deliberately but without force) with the toe of the foot until second gear is felt to engage. Then engage the clutch, but do not remove the toe from the pedal until the clutch is *fully* engaged. Immediately afterwards open the throttle again to maintain speed.

Changing Up into Third Gear (and Fourth Gear on Later Models). Repeat the procedure used for obtaining second gear, but change up into top gear on 3-speed models when you attain a road speed of 20–25 m.p.h. For 4-speed models, change into third gear at about 20 m.p.h. and into top gear at about 25/30 m.p.h.

To Change Down. Throttle down until your Bantam is running at a speed normal for the gear to be selected. Now disengage the clutch, open the throttle slightly, pause a second, and *depress* the gear-change pedal to its *full* extent until the lower gear is *felt* to engage. Avoid the use of any force, but employ a smart action of the foot. As soon as the gear is felt to engage, gently let in the clutch, and remove your toe from the pedal. Then adjust the throttle opening according to the road speed required. Repeat this procedure for each downward gearchange.

Changing Down from Top to First Gear. Except when climbing a gradient it is not essential to complete each of the gear changes individually. You can instead use this procedure: first reduce your speed to a crawl by closing the throttle and applying the front and rear brakes; then disengage the clutch and depress the foot gear-change pedal to its full extent twice (three times on a four-speed gearbox) in quick succession, "blipping" the engine slightly prior to each movement of the pedal. This procedure sounds difficult but in practice is easily mastered. When first gear is felt to engage, engage the clutch, remove the toe from the gear-change pedal, and open the throttle as required.

To Stop in Neutral. Close the throttle almost completely, apply the front and rear brakes together, disengage the clutch and change down into first or second gear. Then with the machine stationary, the engine running slowly and the clutch disengaged, obtain neutral from first or second gear by *slightly* raising or depressing respectively the gear-change pedal.

To stop the engine itself, switch off the ignition by means of the ignition key or switch, according to model. Where an ignition switch is not provided it is necessary to close the throttle completely to stop the engine. Alternatively turn off the petrol tap. Do this before leaving the machine for an extended period so that the petroil mixture is thereby drained from the carburettor float chamber, thus obviating the risk of oil settling in the float chamber while the machine is left standing.

Technique of Good Gear Changing. Continue to practise gear changing until the changes can be effected silently, positively, and quickly. Avoid excessive noise, and remember that listening to the rise and fall in the exhaust note considerably facilitates good gear changing. Operate the throttle twist-grip, clutch, and gear-change pedal in one well co-ordinated movement keeping the eyes straight ahead when making each change.

During each gear change keep a steady pressure on the gear-change pedal until the clutch is *fully* engaged. To avoid undue wear and tear, do not let the engine labour in top gear. Always change down *before* the engine gets "bothered" and do not rev-up the engine excessively with a lower gear engaged. The Bantam gearbox is sturdy, but always treat it with some respect. You will then find that it will operate efficiently without any attention to its mechanism for a very big mileage. For information on gearbox lubrication, *see* page 18.

Steering Lock (1956–70 Models). Mounted beneath the bottom fork-yoke on 1956–9 Bantams, this has a key. To lock the steering, turn the forks to the *left* and then turn the key *anti-clockwise* in the lock to release the plunger. The machine is then safe from being wheeled or ridden away. Always keep the key on a chain ring to prevent loss. On 1960–70 models no plunger and key are provided and a padlock should be used for locking purposes. Turn the forks to the left until the hole in the special frame lug coincides with a corresponding hole in the bottom yoke lug. Then lock the two lugs together with a padlock.

Ministry of Transport Test Certificate. A MoT certificate for road worthiness must be obtained from an authorized garage, dealer or repair shop in respect of any motor-cycle used in the U.K. which was first registered *more than three years ago*. Subsequently the certificate must be renewed *annually*. It must be produced when applying for a registration licence in respect of renewal or change of ownership (Forms VE 1/A and VE 1/2 respectively), together with a valid *certificate of insurance* and the registration book.

The MoT certificate costs 87½p and it is legal to ride an *untaxed* motor-cycle to a suitable testing station after making an appointment for a test there. The required certificate is issued on the spot if the motor-cycle passes the statutory test for efficiency of the tyres, brakes, steering, lamps, horn, etc.

2 Bantam lubrication

ENGINE LUBRICATION

The basic purpose of all engine lubrication systems is to prevent friction (and consequent heat) between all moving surfaces by creating an oil film between these moving surfaces and thereby preventing damaging metal-to-metal contact. To ensure efficient lubrication it is necessary to:

1. Use a suitable brand and grade of engine oil.
2. See that the petroil mixture in the tank contains the correct proportions of oil and petrol.
3. Drain off occasionally any liquid oil accumulated in the crankcase. Do not coast downhill for long with the *throttle shut*.

The Petroil Lubrication System. This is the simplest form of two-stroke engine lubrication system, highly efficient and requiring the minimum of attention on the part of the owner rider. With this system the engine oil is mixed with the fuel in the tank in definite proportions (*see* later paragraph) and this petroil mixture is fed to the carburettor and sucked into the crankcase via the inlet port during each upward piston stroke. As the piston descends the petroil mixture is compressed in the crankcase and most of the oil is separated out as liquid oil which gets on the crankshaft assembly and splash-lubricates the various internal moving parts (assisted by a fan-type impeller, 1956–66).

The petrol and air components of the petroil mixture pass up through the transfer port into the combustion chamber. Surplus engine oil is carried by the transfer of fuel into the combustion chamber. Later D1, D5, D7, D7D/L engines (with caged roller big-end bearing) have a positive oil feed for the mainshaft bearings (*see* Fig. 10)

Suitable Engine Oils. It is most desirable always to purchase engine oil in sealed containers or from branded cabinets and never to buy an inferior or unsuitable oil, otherwise you may be landed with a worn or damaged cylinder, piston, bearings, etc. If you must economize, cut down on cigarettes, not engine oil. B.S.A. Motor Cycles Ltd. recommended the use of one of the following oils, for summer and winter use:

1. Castrol Two-stroke Oil.
2. Mobiloil Mobilix TT.

3. Esso Two-stroke (2T) Motor Oil.
4. Energol Two-stroke Oil.
5. Shell 2T Two-stroke Oil.
6. Regent Motor Oil 2T.

Self-mixing Engine Oils. The first five of the above oils are specially prepared for two-stroke engines and dissolve very quickly and completely with the petrol.

The Petroil Mixture. It is essential that the petroil mixture consists of the correct proportions of petrol and engine oil.

In 1967 the proportion of petrol and self-mixing oil was changed as a result of the development of improved oils for use in two-stroke engines and shortly afterwards the oil measure hitherto incorporated in the filler cap was discontinued.

Although all earlier Bantams were supplied with an oil measure, the dimensions of which varied according to model and various mixture strengths quoted for different purposes, the latest recommendations are suitable for all models. Hence cap markings can be ignored.

Recommended petroil mixture (by volume) using one of the specially prepared two-stroke engine oils quoted above, is as follows

1 part oil to 24 parts petrol (i.e. a 4 per cent mixture)

The majority of garage petroil dispensers are designed to give variable proportions, so make sure that the attendant has set the controls to give the correct ratio.

It is always important to ensure that during replenishment, the petrol and oil are thoroughly mixed. If the oil is not properly absorbed in the petrol, there is considerable risk of undiluted oil reaching the carburettor jet, with consequent difficulty in starting.

For those owners who prefer to mix their own petroil using "standard" oil, or are unable to obtain ready-mixed fuel containing the special two-stroke lubricating oil, an engine oil of SAE 40 grade must be used, the proportions of the mixture being 1 part oil to 32 parts petrol (or a 3 per cent mixture). In these circumstances, it is preferable to have the petrol in a separate container, add the right amount of engine oil, and shake thoroughly until the oil is completely dissolved in the petrol. Only then should the petroil be put into your Bantam tank. It will also be advisable before starting up, especially after standing overnight, to agitate the fuel in the tank by rocking the machine sideways. This will avoid the possibility of neat oil (which may have settled in the bottom of the tank) passing direct to the carburettor, making starting difficult, if not impossible. It must be emphasized that the manufacturers strongly recommend the use of the special two-stroke engine oils and every effort should be made to obtain these lubricants. Use the SAE 40 grade of engine oil only when the recommended engine oils cannot be obtained.

Suitable grades of SAE 40 engine oils are: Castrol XXL; Shell X100–40; Esso Motor Oil 40/50; Mobiloil "A"; Energol SAE 40; Havoline SAE 40.

Draining the Crankcase. It is seldom that any appreciable quantity of liquid engine oil accumulates in the crankcase, but when such oil is present it should be drained off. Do this preferably after a run, when the engine is warm and the oil flows freely, thus clearing any impurities or deposits within the crankcase. During the running-in period (1,500 miles) it is particularly important to drain the crankcase, as this eradicates any minute metallic particles collected therein and produced by the bedding down of bearings, piston rings, etc.

The makers of the Bantam strongly advise draining the crankcase of a new or reconditioned engine after covering approximately 250 miles (400 km) and again at 1,000 miles. Subsequently, draining at intervals of about 2,000 miles (3,200 km) should be quite sufficient. To drain the crankcase remove the *smaller* of the two screwed plugs from the base of the crankcase after placing a drip tray or dish beneath the engine, and allow all accumulated oil to drain off. When oil ceases to drip, replace the drain plug and washer, and make quite sure that the drain plug is tightened securely. Remember that on a two-stroke engine a crankcase leakage will result in loss of compression.

Draining the Gearbox. Although the engine and gearbox embody unit construction, and the gearbox is essentially a part of the power unit, the

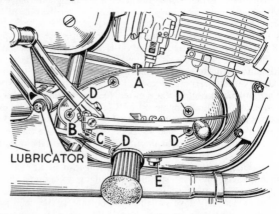

Fig. 7. The primary drive chain-case

A. *Gearbox filler plug*
B. *Nut securing kick-starter crank*
C. *Nut securing gear-change lever*

D. *Cheese-headed screws (five) securing primary drive chain-case cover*
E. *Gearbox drain plug*

gearbox is from a lubrication point of view entirely separate. It is advisable when draining the crankcase (*see* previous paragraph) also to drain and flush out the gearbox. Except during the running-in period, draining and flushing about every 2,000 miles is sufficient.

To drain the gearbox, remove the *larger* of the two plugs beneath the gearbox (the plug is shown at *E* in Fig. 7) and allow the whole of the old oil to drain off into a suitable receptacle. Then flush out the gearbox with a suitable flushing oil, and refill it with new oil (*see* below) to the level of the dipstick graduation (*see below*). The capacity of the gearbox is ¾ pint (425 cm³), except for four-speed gearboxes, when the capacity is 1 pint (570 cm³).

Suitable Gearbox Oils. Self-mixing engine oils should *not* be used for gearbox lubrication. They should be of grade SAE 40. Six suitable oils to use (summer and winter) are:

1. Castrol XXL.
2. Mobiloil BB.
3. Esso Extra Motor Oil 40/50.
4. B.P. Energol SAE 40.
5. Shell X–100 SAE 40.
6. Regent Havoline SAE 40.

Top-up the Gearbox Every 1,000 Miles. Remove the filler plug, *A*, Fig. 7, and check the oil level in the gearbox. If necessary, top-up with one of the six engine oils mentioned above so that the level just reaches to the bottom of the dipstick attached to the filler plug, when the latter is *placed* in position over the filler-plug orifice. When the filler plug is screwed fully home, the oil level will then reach the graduation (showing the correct oil level) on the dipstick.

With the introduction of the four-speed gearbox, one of the chaincase cover drain screws *D*, Fig. 7 (coloured red) adjacent to the footrest is utilized to determine the oil level.

Remove the screw and filler plug *A*, adding oil until it flows from the level hole. Replace the screw as soon as surplus oil has drained away, and re-fit the filler plug.

Primary Chain Lubrication. The chain is enclosed within the chain-case on the off-side of the power unit (*see* Fig. 52), and provided that the gearbox is kept topped-up correctly, the chain as well as the gearbox contents is adequately lubricated. Both have a common oil supply. (*See* also Fig. 10.)

The Oil-dip Air Cleaner (1948–60). 1948–60 Bantams have an oil-dip type air cleaner built into the intake bell of the Amal carburettor. About every 1,000 miles (1,500 km) release the clip bolt and detach the bell. Allow it to soak thoroughly in petrol, dry it out, and then submerge in light engine oil for several minutes. Remove the bell, drain off all surplus oil, dry the bell externally, and finally replace it on the carburettor.

The Air Cleaner (1961–6). The air cleaner is built into the air intake bell of the carburettor and should be dismantled and cleaned about every 1,000 miles. Release the clip bolt and remove the bell. Soak it thoroughly in petrol, allow to dry, and reassemble.

The Air Cleaner (1967). The air cleaner is of the "pill-box" type and unscrews from the carburettor. Release the clip bolt, remove the perforated band and the filter element. Wash this thoroughly in petrol and dry thoroughly before replacing. Great care is necessary when screwing the air cleaner on to the carburettor because the threads are shallow and easily "crossed." This problem is aggravated by the comparatively soft material of which the carburettor is made.

The Air Cleaner (1968–70). The felt element is concealed by the right-side panel and is retained by a flexible strap. After removal, wash in petrol, allow to dry, and replace.

Special Note for Air Cleaners. Regular servicing is essential, otherwise the cleaner will become choked, resulting in heavy petrol consumption, poor performance, and excessive wear of the cylinder walls, due to an over-rich mixture at the carburettor.

Contact-breaker Lubrication. Where Wipac electrical equipment is provided, the contact-breaker requires little attention. Every 5,000 miles (4,500 km) remove the cam lubricating-pad (*see* Figs. 18, 19, 20 and 21) and smear it lightly with a little high-melting-point grease. On machines with Lucas electrical equipment (1950–3) smear a few drops of engine oil every 3,000 miles on the felt lubricator shown at *E* in Fig. 22. Also withdraw the contact-breaker rocker arm and smear a trace of grease or engine oil on the contact-breaker rocker arm pivot *C*.

THE MOTOR CYCLE PARTS

Although engine lubrication is of paramount importance, never neglect to lubricate the motor-cycle parts *regularly*. For most lubrication points a grease gun is required, but certain items need attention with an oil can.

Suitable Greases. Six suitable greases, recommended by B.S.A. Motor Cycles Ltd. are:
1. Castrolease L.M.
2. Shell Retinax A.
3. Esso Multi Purpose Grease H.
4. B.P. Energrease L2.
5. Mobilgrease MP.
6. Regent Marfak Multi purpose 2.
All the above greases possess excellent lubrication properties.

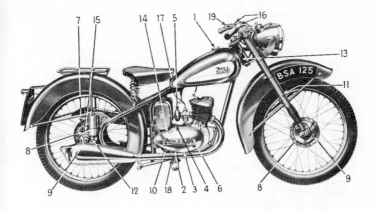

Fig. 8. When and where to lubricate your Bantam

A 1952 spring-frame Model D1 is shown above. With few exceptions, the lubrication points indicated are similar on all models.

1. **Petroil tank.** *Replenish with a 24 to 1 mixture of petrol and engine oil. The petrol and oil must be thoroughly mixed (see page 17)*
2. **Crankcase.** *Drain after the first 250 miles, at 1,000 miles, and subsequently at intervals of 2,000 miles (see page 18)*
3. **Gearbox.** *Drain, flush out, and replenish with new engine oil at 250 miles, 1,000 miles, and thereafter at 2,000 miles (see page 18)*
4. **Gearbox.** *Top-up every 1,000 miles with engine oil to the level indicated on the dipstick or level screw hole (see page 19)*
5. **Air cleaner.** *Every 1,000 miles remove and clean thoroughly (see page 20)*
6. **Contact-breaker.** *If Wico-Pacy, grease cam lubricating pad every 5,000 miles. If Lucas, oil felt cam-lubricator and rocker-arm pivot every 3,000 miles (see page 20)*
7. **Secondary Chain.** *Oil or grease chain regularly. Periodically remove, clean and immerse in mixture of grease and graphite (see page 22)*
8. **Wheel hubs.** *Grease every 1,000 miles where nipples are provided (see page 22). These were discontinued on later models.*
9. **Brake-cam spindles.** *Oil every 1,000 miles, grease every 2,000 miles (see page 23)*
10. **Rear brake pedal.** *Oil shaft weekly (see page 23)*
11. **Front forks.** *Grease both nipples where provided every 1,000 miles (see page 23). On D7, D10, D14, and Bantam 175 models renew oil in fork legs when necessary (see page 23)*
12. **Plunger suspension units.** *Grease both nipples every 1,000 miles (see page 24). On Models D7, D10, D14, and Bantam 175 grease swinging arm pivot nipples*
13. **Steering head.** *Apply grease gun to single nipple (where provided) every 1,000 miles (see page 24)*
14. **Clutch withdrawal mechanism.** *Grease nipple every 1,000 miles (see page 24)*
15. **Speedometer drive.** *Grease gearbox every 2,000 miles (see page 24)*
16. **Control cables and levers.** *Oil weekly (see page 25)*
17. **Saddle-nose bolt.** *Oil every 1,000 miles (see page 25) Early models only.*
18. **Central stand.** *Oil every 1,000 miles (see page 25)*
19. **Dipper switch.** *Oil every 5,000 miles (see page 9)*
20. **Stop–tail lamp switch** *(not shown). Oil occasionally*

Lubrication of Secondary Chain. No automatic lubrication of the secondary chain is provided, and whenever the chain appears to be running somewhat dry, apply an oil-can to the lower chain run while slowly turning the rear wheel by hand. Alternatively smear some grease on the chain with a stiff brush.

It is advisable periodically (say every 2,500–3,000 miles) to remove the chain and submerge it in a paraffin bath. Permit the chain to soak well, so that all dirt is removed, and then hang the chain up to dry. Afterwards thoroughly grease or oil the chain. Preferably it should be immersed for about five minutes in a suitable receptacle containing a warm mixture of grease and graphite. Then allow all surplus to drain off the chain. Finally fit the chain to the gearbox and rear-wheel sprockets. In doing this, make sure that the spring link is replaced with the open end facing *away from* the direction of chain movement.

Grease Hubs Every 1,000 Miles (D1, D3 and D5 Models). Apply the grease gun to the nipples on the front and rear hubs about every 1,000 miles (1,500 km), using three to four strokes. Be careful not to over-lubricate the hubs, or grease may penetrate to the brake linings and seriously reduce

Fig. 9. Showing rear hub speedometer drive
Grease the nipple shown at A about every 2,000 miles

braking efficiency. On no account use engine oil, this being too thin for the heavy duty roller bearings. On Models D7, D10, D14, and Bantam 175 the ball journal bearings are packed with grease during initial assembly and this should suffice until a complete overhaul is necessary.

Oil Brake-cam Spindles. At the same time as you lubricate the hubs (i.e. at 1,000 mile intervals), apply an oil-can to the brake-cam spindle lubricators. Only a few drops of oil are needed. On Models D5, D7, D10, D14, and Bantam 175, apply grease every 2,000 miles, using one stroke only of the grease gun. This is important, because excessive lubrication may cause the brake linings to become contaminated with grease, seriously reducing braking efficiency.

The Rear-brake Pedal. Weekly lubricate with a few drops of oil the rear-brake pedal shaft. Also oil the brake linkage.

Lubrication of Front Forks (Models D1, D3, D5). A grease nipple is provided on each telescopic front-fork leg for the lubrication of the sliding members, and it is advisable to apply the grease gun to it every 1,000 miles, giving a few strokes of the gun. Apart from the two grease nipples the forks have no other lubrication points requiring attention.

Lubrication of Front Forks (Models D7, D10, D14, and Bantam 175). No grease nipples are provided and the only lubrication necessary is renewal of the oil in the fork legs after a considerable mileage. The need for renewing the oil is indicated by excessive fork movement. Suitable oils to use are: Shell Motor Oil 101, Esso 10W/30, Mobil Super, Castrolite, B.P.

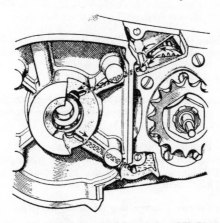

Fig. 10. On the 1958–9 Model D5 and the 1958–70 Models D1, D7, D10, D14, and Bantam 175, the gearbox and primary chain case oil automatically lubricates the crankshaft left- and right-side bearings respectively

Surplus oil drains back into the primary chain-case
(By courtesy of "Motor Cycle," London)

Energol 10W/40, and Regent Havoline 10W/30. Oil renewal for each leg should be effected in the following manner.

Prise out the cap on the top of each fork leg by means of the small hole provided, and with a tubular spanner unscrew the small nut exposed. Next remove the large nut which carried the cap. Then disconnect the mudguard stay and unscrew the stud which is also the lower mudguard connection. Allow all oil to drain out. Then apply the front brake and depress the forks a few times to drain out any remaining oil. Replace the drain stud and fibre washer and add ⅛ pint of one of the above-mentioned oils to each fork leg. Finally replace the top nuts and cap.

The 1968 D14 Bantam Sports and all 1969–70 D14 models were fitted with new forks based on the design of those used on the larger machines. A drain screw is provided at the bottom of each leg and the oil can be renewed after unscrewing the large cap nut on top of the fork leg. When draining, remove the cap nut first and, after the drain plug has been taken out, apply the front brake and "pump" the forks up and down a few times to make sure the legs are quite empty. Replace the drain screw, re-fill with 175 cm³ of oil from the above list, firmly tightening the cap nut afterwards. The quantity of oil quoted is a little less than ⅛ pint.

Plunger Suspension Units (Models D1, D3). Each unit has one grease nipple. Apply the grease gun every 1,000 miles (a few strokes). It is important to lubricate the rear-suspension units regularly, as this gives maximum comfort and reduces any tendency for the lower tubular members to rust.

Rear Suspension (Models D5, D7, D10, D14, and Bantam 175). The two suspension units which are sealed during manufacture require no lubrication. The swinging arm pivot has lubricators (*see* Fig. 7) and the grease-gun should be applied every 1,000 miles.

Grease Steering Head Every 1,000 Miles (D1, D3 and D5 models). A few strokes of the grease gun to the nipple low down on the near side of the head is all that is necessary.

The Clutch Withdrawal Mechanism. To ensure smooth and positive operation of the clutch, it is important to apply the grease gun about every 1,000 miles (1,500 km) to the grease nipple on the near side just above the clutch-control adjustment (*see* Figs. 6 and 56).

Folding Kick-starter (Competition Models). Lubricate the pivot pin occasionally with engine oil.

The Speedometer Drive. The drive for the speedometer is taken off the rear hub, and a grease nipple for lubricating the speedometer gearbox on the off side is provided (*see* Fig. 9). Apply the grease gun about every 2,000 miles. Give a few strokes.

Oil Control Cables and Levers Weekly. Apply an oil-can (engine oil) to the handlebar levers, and do not omit to lubricate the ends of the operating cables which are subjected to considerable stresses. Also oil all external linkages to ensure free movement and reduce rusting. A few drops of oil are quite sufficient. Little and often is the best policy.

Saddle-nose Bolt. Apply every 1,000 miles a few drops of engine oil to the saddle-nose bolt (except where a dualseat is fitted).

The Central Stand. Apply a few drops of engine oil every 1,000 miles to the stand pivots.

The Steering Lock (1956–9 D3, D5, D7). Do not insert oil into the key-hole, for this is apt to clog the wards and disperse the specially prepared lubricant used during the initial assembly of the steering lock. It is permissible, however, after a big mileage and when riding continuously in wet weather to apply a few drops of *thin machine oil* to the periphery of the moving drum.

3 Correct carburation

The purpose of the carburettor is to supply the crankcase and the combustion chamber (via the transfer ports) with a correctly proportioned mixture (about 13 parts of air to 1 of petrol). The mixture on the Bantam also contains oil mist which is deposited in the crankcase during downward piston strokes.

Once the carburettor is correctly tuned it requires very little attention. The maker's settting is suitable for big temperature variations and road conditions, and it is rarely necessary to interfere with this setting. So long as the engine runs well it is best to leave the carburettor well alone, except for occcasional cleaning. Circumstances may, however, arise where it is desirable to alter the setting.

The Instrument Fitted. The carburettor fitted to the D1, D3 Bantams is a standard clip-fitted needle-controlled single-jet Amal instrument, and its official type number is 261/001D on the 1948–50 models. On the 1951–63 D1, D3 Bantams the carburettor number is 361/1 (223/7 on the 148 cm³ models). The essential difference between the carburettor fitted to 1948–50 models and that specified on 1951–63 models is that in the former case the float-chamber cover screws into the chamber, whereas in the latter instance the the float-chamber cover is secured by two pins.

Twist-grip throttle control is provided and control of the carburettor air-strangler is by a small lever on the strangler itself. The carburettor has a semi-automatic action, and it is necessary to close the strangler or air slide (according to model) only when starting up from cold (*see* page 4). For comprehensive details of the "Monobloc" carburettor used on models D5 and D7 *see* page 32, and for details of the "Concentric" carburettor used on models D10, D14, and Bantam 175, *see* page 32.

STANDARD CARBURETTOR DETAILS

Before considering the actual tuning of the Amal carburettor, it is desirable to discuss briefly the various components which are directly concerned with tuning.

The Main Jet. The main jet (shown at (21) and A in Figs. 11, 12, respectively) does not affect the slow-running, or tick-over mixture, but it regulates the maximum supply of petroil from the *half to full throttle* positions. Every Amal main jet is carefully calibrated for fuel flow, and you will observe a number stamped on its hexagon. This is an indication of the volume of petroil which can flow through the main jet orifice in a given time. Note that the jet numbers are in multiples of five, e.g. 25, 30, 35, 40, 45, 50, 55, etc., and the higher the jet number, the greater is the flow capacity of the jet. When you buy a new jet, see that it has a seal attached. This seal guarantees that the size of the jet is in accordance with the number stamped on it. On no account attempt to ream out the jet orifice.

The Throttle Slide. The throttle valve or slide shown at (15) in Figs. 11, 11A is cable-controlled from the throttle twist-grip and from the fully closed to fully open position increases progressively the volume of gas sucked into the crankcase. Every throttle slide has a cut-away portion or slope as indicated at *J* in Fig. 11A. Throttle slides with different cut-aways are available and each particular cut-away has a number stamped at the base. Note that the bigger the cut-away and corresponding number, the weaker is the petroil mixture for slow-runnning (idling) and up to the half-throttle position. The same of course holds good for the half-throttle position to the slow-running position.

The Jet-needle. The needle shown at (19) in Figs. 11, 11A is secured to the throttle slide by the spring clip shown at (14) in Fig. 11 and therefore works up and down with the throttle slide. The tapered portion of the needle also moves similarly in the needle-jet shown at (18) in Fig. 11, and thereby regulates the admission of petrol vapour at different throttle openings. As may be seen in Fig. 11A, several grooves are provided on the needle, and the fitting of the clip (14) into different grooves will affect the mixture. Note that No. 1 groove is that near the end of the non-tapered part of the needle. No. 1 groove provides the lowest needle position and the weakest mixture. The effect of raising the needle by using groove No. 2, 3, or 4 is to enrich the mixture. In Fig. 11A, the spring clip is shown in groove position 2.

The Needle-jet. This is shown at (18) in Fig. 11. No marking is used on the standard size jet, but other size jets are obtainable and these are marked accordingly. Note that if the mixture becomes over-rich at half throttle after a very big mileage has been covered, it is probable that the bore of the needle-jet has worn, and the jet requires to be renewed. If the slow-running mixture is very weak, this may be corrected by fitting a larger bore needle-jet, if a smaller cut-away and raising of the needle do not effect a cure.

The Carburettor Strangler. As has been mentioned on page 4, the carburettor strangler is normally closed only when starting up the engine from cold. The effect of closing the strangler is to cut down the air supply and

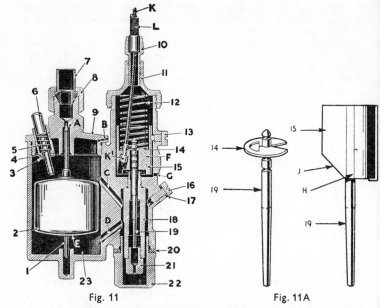

Fig. 11

Fig. 11A

Fig. 11. Diagrammatic section through Amal standard type single-jet carburettor

Note that on type 361 carburettors a spring bow is fastened to the float at E and secures the
float needle to the float. Type 261 carburettors have a one-piece float and needle as shown.
The anchorage K¹ of the cable K is actually in front of the jet, not as shown

Fig. 11A. Amal throttle slide and jet-needle

A. Float-needle seating
B. Float-chamber air vent
C. Air release duct
D. Petroil duct to main jet
E. Location for spring bow on type 361 carburettor
F. Choke bore

G. Mixing-chamber drain hole (to counteract flooding)
H. Throttle-slide guide groove
J. Throttle-slide cut-away
K. Throttle cable (to twist-grip)
K¹. Throttle-cable nipple
L. Cable casing

1. Float needle
2. Float
3. Cotter for tickler
4. Bush for tickler
5. Tickler return-spring
6. Tickler
7. Fuel-pipe union nipple
8. Fuel-pipe union nut
9. Float-chamber cover
10. Throttle-cable adjuster
11. Mixing-chamber cap
12. Throttle-spring

13. Locating screw for throttle slide
14. Spring clip securing tapered needle to throttle slide
15. Throttle slide
16. Feed-hole screw
17. Washer for feed-hole screw
18. Needle-jet
19. Tapered jet-needle
20. Washer for jet plug
21. Main jet
22. Jet plug
23. Float chamber

increase the suction on the jet. When tuning the carburettor, however, it may be very helpful to close the strangler experimentally for a brief period in order to find out the effect of enriching the mixture.

ADJUSTMENT (STANDARD CARBURETTOR)

Permissible Adjustment. B.S.A. Motor Cycles Ltd. emphasize that no alteration to the carburettor setting should be made except for special requirements, and then preferably on expert advice. If the conditions of running are such that it is felt that greater economy of fuel can be obtained, try the effect of fitting a slightly smaller main jet A (Fig. 12). Alternatively lower the jet needle B *one notch*. Note that the fitting of a smaller size main jet will weaken the mixture slightly throughout the entire range of throttle openings, but the lowering of the jet-needle will weaken the mixture only on intermediate throttle openings. Full throttle openings will be unaffected.

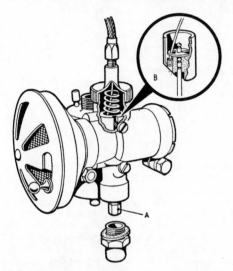

Fig. 12. Standard carburettor with jet plug removed
A. *Main jet*   B. *Jet needle*

If the engine is running on an obviously weak mixture, you can try the effect of fitting a slightly larger main jet or raising the jet-needle *one notch*. The former adjustment will enrich the mixture throughout the entire throttle range, while the latter adjustment will affect intermediate throttle openings only.

Table I
STANDARD CARBURETTOR SETTINGS FOR 1948–63
TWO-STROKE BANTAMS (SEE ALSO PAGES 39 AND 42)

Bantam model	Carburettor type No.	Main jet	Throttle valve	Needle-jet	Needle position
D1 (1948–50)	261/001D	75	5	0·106	2
D1 (1951–63)	361/1	75	5	0·106	2
D3 (1954–7)	223/7	95	5	0·1075	2

MAINTENANCE (STANDARD CARBURETTOR)

Dismantling Carburettor. This is quite straightforward. To obtain access to the main jet and the needle-jet into which it is screwed, it is only necessary to unscrew the jet plug (as shown in Fig. 12) from the base of the mixing chamber. Both jets can then be removed.

To remove the throttle slide and the tapered needle attached to it, unscrew the mixing-chamber cap and withdraw the throttle slide and jet-needle. Note that the locating screw (13) (*see* Fig. 11) engages a groove in the throttle slide and guides the slide.

To release the throttle operating-cable, detach the cable from the slot in the throttle slide. To remove the float and attached needle from the float chamber, remove the float-chamber cover (*see* page 28) and withdraw them from the top of the float chamber. To remove the carburettor strangler from the air intake, slacken the clip securing-bolt and pull the assembly away.

Attention to Float Chamber. Impurities which collect in the float chamber are a frequent cause of persistent flooding, and it is therefore important to clean the float chamber every few months. Detach the petrol pipe from the float chamber cover, remove the cover, also the float, and carefully clean out all passages. Check that the needle, integral with the float or secured to it by a spring bow, is not bent. A bent needle will cause the float to stick and thereby cause flooding. Also shake the float to ascertain that no petrol has entered it as the result of a small puncture or a damaged seam.

If persistent flooding occurs in spite of the float chamber being clean, and the needle is not bent or the float punctured, it is probable that the float needle is not seating properly. Insert the tapered end of the needle in its seating and rotate it lightly backwards and forwards between the thumb and finger, as though grinding-in a valve. But never use any grinding compound. Should a deep groove be observed on the tapered end of the float needle, renewal of the needle (and float if integral) is called for.

Before replacing the float-chamber cover make sure that the tickler springs back and works freely. Check that the air vent in the rim of the cover is unobstructed. When replacing the float-chamber cover, first check that the blunt end of the float needle is located in the guide hole at the base of the float chamber, and then before securing the float-chamber cover, carefully guide the cover over the tapered end of the needle.

Wear of Throttle Slide and Needle-jet. After a very big mileage the throttle slide may become worn and a slack fit in the barrel of the mixing chamber. Such wear will cause air leaks and interfere with good slow-running, and the remedy, of course, is to renew the throttle slide.

Bear in mind that a badly worn throttle slide will permit lateral movement of the tapered needle in the needle-jet. The needle itself is of hardened steel and does not wear, but the lateral movement of the needle will gradually widen the bore of the needle jet, thus enriching the mixture and increasing the fuel consumption. The remedy is to lower the tapered jet-needle one notch in the throttle slide (*see* Fig. 11A), or better still, to renew the needle-jet.

Slackness of Air Strangler. Verify that the air strangler when fully opened does in fact *remain* fully open. If the perforated plate is inclined to be slack, slightly bend it so as to make its movement more stiff.

Fit of Carburettor on Inlet Pipe. After the carburettor has been removed from the inlet pipe, it is important when replacing it to make certain that the instrument is pushed fully home on the inlet pipe before spannering the nut which tightens the securing clip (D1, D3). The carburettor must always be a good push-fit on the inlet pipe and should be pushed home true with a screwing action after smearing some oil on the inlet pipe. Slackness or excessive tightness must always be avoided.

If the Mixture is Weak. The usual symptoms of a weak mixture are: erratic slow-running; poor acceleration; spitting back in the carburettor; overheating of the engine; a tendency for the engine to run poorly at full throttle openings; and greyness and dryness of the sparking plug points. If the engine ticks-over better after depressing the float tickler and delivers greater power with the air strangler partly closed, the mixture is undoubtedly weak.

Some possible causes of a weak mixture are: air leaks at the crankcase joint; a partial obstruction in the main jet or fuel supply; fuel accidently contaminated with water; a main jet which is too small; an incorrect jet-needle position (needle too low in throttle slide).

If the Mixture is Rich. The accompanying symptoms are generally as follows: a tendency for the engine to indulge in four-stroking; spraying of fuel from the carburettor; high fuel consumption; black (sooty) smoke issuing from the silencer; heavy "lumpy" running of the engine; and quick sooting-up of the sparking plug. If tick-over is better with the fuel tap shut temporarily, and spitting-back disappears on opening the throttle quickly (with the engine cold), the mixture is certainly rich.

Possible causes of a rich mixture include: sticking of the float tickler; a main jet which is too large or not screwed right home; a needle-jet whose bore has increased in size through wear; an incorrect jet-needle position (needle too high in throttle slide); flooding (*see* page 30).

"MONOBLOC" CARBURETTOR DETAILS

The Pilot Air-adjusting Screw. This adjusting screw, shown at (29) in Fig. 13, regulates the suction imposed on the pilot jet, shown at (9) in Fig. 14, by controlling the volume of air which mixes with the petrol. It controls the mixture strength for idling and also for initial throttle openings (up to one-eighth throttle).

The Throttle Stop. The throttle-stop screw, shown at (30) in Fig. 14, is normally adjusted to prop the throttle valve open sufficiently to enable the engine to tick-over nicely when the throttle twist-grip is fully closed. To obtain good slow running a combined adjustment of the throttle-stop screw and the pilot air-adjusting screw is required.

The Main Jet. This jet, shown at (13) in Fig. 14, controls the fuel supply at throttle openings exceeding three-quarters open. At smaller throttle openings the fuel supplied passes through the main jet, but the amount is decreased owing to the needle in the needle-jet, shown at (15)

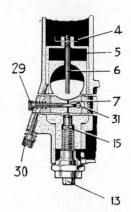

Fig. 13. Showing the throttle-stop and pilot air adjusting screw for slow-running adjustment

For key to numbered parts, see page 35

in Fig. 14 having a controlling effect. The main jet is screwed into the needle-jet and can readily be withdrawn after removing the main-jet cover nut shown at (12) in Fig. 14.

Each Amal main jet is numbered and calibrated so that its precise discharge is known. Thus it follows that any two main jets having the same number are identical in all respects. The larger the jet, the higher is its number. It is not advisable to use a main jet larger than the size recommended by B.S.A. Motor Cycles Ltd.

The Jet-needle and Needle-jet. The jet-needle, shown at (6) in Fig. 13 is attached to, and moves with, the throttle valve. Being tapered, it permits more or less fuel to pass through the needle-jet, shown at (15) in Fig. 13, as the throttle is opened or closed respectively. This applies throughout the range of throttle openings, except at full throttle and when idling. The needle-jet is of a specified size, and this should not be changed.

As may be seen in Fig. 13, the position of the jet-needle (6) relative to the throttle opening can be adjusted according to the mixture required by securing the needle to the throttle valve with the needle spring-clip (4) in a particular groove, five of which are provided. Position 3, for example, means the *third groove from the top*. At throttle openings from one-quarter to three-quarters open *raising* the needle *enriches* the mixture, while *lowering* the needle *weakens* it. The needle itself is made in one size only, and its position should not normally be changed.

MAINTENANCE ("MONOBLOC" CARBURETTOR)

Altering Slow-running Adjustment. The adjustment should be made with the engine already *warmed up*. If slow running is poor, screw home the pilot air-adjusting screw and then unscrew it (usually about *two* complete turns) until the engine idles at an excessive speed, with the throttle twist-grip closed and the throttle valve abutting the throttle-stop screw. The air strangler or air control (1966 models) should be fully open.

Referring to Fig. 13, unscrew the throttle-stop screw (30) until the engine slows up and begins to falter. Then screw the pilot air-adjusting screw (29) in or out as required to enable the engine to run regularly and faster. To *weaken* the mixture, screw the pilot air-adjusting screw *outwards*.

Slowly lower the throttle-stop screw until the engine again commences to falter. Then re-set the pilot air-adjusting screw to obtain the best slow running. If after making this second adjustment the engine ticks-over too fast, repeat the adjustment a third time. The combined adjustment sounds complicated, but in practice it is quite simple. It is important to avoid excessive richness of the slow-running mixture, especially if much riding is done on small throttle openings. If the mixture is too rich, considerable running on the pilot jet will occur while riding, with consequently a high fuel consumption.

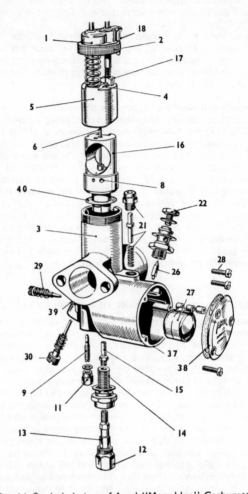

Fig. 14. Exploded view of Amal "Monobloc" Carburettor

A key to the numbered parts of the carburettor is given opposite. This carburettor is fitted to the 1958–66 Models D5, D7, D7D/L (B.S.A. Motor Cycles Ltd.)

Aim at obtaining the best tick-over at a *moderate speed* with a mixture bordering on the weak side. The engine should be on the point of "spitting-back." Too slow a tick-over is not recommended as this can cause insufficient lubrication of the cylinder bore while the engine is hot. An excessively fast tick-over speed should be avoided as this causes overheating and excessive noise.

Persistent Poor Slow Running. If poor slow running continues after making a careful slow-running adjustment as previously described, the cause may be one or more of the following:

1. An obstructed pilot jet.
2. Air leaks caused through a poor joint between the carburettor flange and cylinder barrel face.
3. A sparking plug which has become dirty or oily or has an incorrect gap between the points.
4. An incorrect contact-breaker gap.
5. Incorrect ignition timing.

To Clear an Obstructed Pilot Jet. The pilot jet has a very narrow fuel passage and can easily become choked. Referring to Fig. 14, to remove the pilot jet (9), remove its cover nut (11) and then unscrew the jet itself. Clean it thoroughly and then blow through it, using the motor-cycle pump. It is also important to see that the air passage to the pilot jet is unobstructed. This should also be blown through. The same applies to the pilot outlet and pilot by-pass passages.

An Abnormally High Petrol Consumption. Sometimes petrol consumption remains high in spite of the carburettor being carefully tuned for

---

Key to Figs. 13–15

1. Mixing-chamber cap
2. Mixing-chamber lock ring
3. Mixing chamber
4. Jet-needle clip
5. Throttle valve
6. Jet-needle (tapered)
7. Pilot outlet
8. Pilot by-pass
9. Pilot jet (detachable)
10. Feed to pilot jet
11. Pilot jet cover nut
12. Main jet cover nut
13. Main jet
14. Main-jet holder
15. Needle-jet
16. Jet block
17. Air valve
18. Locking spring for 2
19. Cable adjuster (air)

20. Cable adjuster (throttle)
21. Tickler assembly
22. Banjo bolt
23. Banjo
24. Nylon filter
25. Needle seating
26. Float-chamber needle
27. Float (hinged)
28. Float-chamber cover screws
29. Pilot air-adjusting screw
30. Throttle-stop screw
31. Air passage to pilot jet
33. "Bleed" holes in 15
36. Throttle-valve cut-away
37. Float chamber
38. Float-chamber cover
39. Locating screw for 16
40. Jet block fibre seal

slow running. There are many possible causes. Some are: leakage from the carburettor due to sticking of the moulded-nylon float needle: a faulty float; a poor float-chamber cover joint; a slack main jet holder or main-jet cover nut; a loose pilot jet; a worn needle-jet; slack petrol pipe union nuts; poor engine compression caused by badly fitting piston rings; binding of the brake shoes on the brake drums; an excessively tight or dry secondary chain; or a slipping clutch. A careful investigation for the cause must be made.

Some less obvious reasons for a high petrol consumption are; air leaks due to a poor joint between the carburettor flange and cylinder barrel or late ignition timing.

Do not attempt to reduce petrol consumption by fitting a smaller size main jet. The size of this jet has no effect unless the motor cycle is being ridden with the throttle more than half open. Where the reason for a high petrol consumption is found difficult or impossible to detect, try lowering the tapered jet-needle attached to the throttle valve *one notch*. See that the jet-needle clip beds home properly in the needle groove.

Dismantling "Monobloc" Carburettor. First see that the petrol tap is closed and disconnect the petrol pipe from the float-chamber union by unscrewing the union nut. Referring to Fig. 14, remove both nuts which secure the carburettor to the cylinder barrel face and unscrew the knurled lock-ring (2) on top of the mixing chamber (3). Then withdraw the carburettor. While removing the carburettor pull the air valve (17), provided on 1966 models. and the throttle valve (5) from the mixing chamber and tie them up temporarily out of the way. Unless it is desired to inspect the slides closely it is not necessary to remove them from their cables. Check that the carburettor flange washer is in good condition.

Further dismantling of the carburettor for cleaning and inspection is straightforward. Again referring to Fig. 14, to remove the jet-needle (6), withdraw the jet-needle clip (4), on top of the throttle valve (5) and remove the needle. To obtain access to the float (27) remove the three screws (28) securing the float-chamber cover (38) to the float chamber (37). Lift out the hinged float (27) and withdraw the moulded-nylon needle (26). Lay both aside for cleaning. The float-chamber vent, by the way, is embodied in the tickler assembly (21), and the top-feed union houses a filter element of nylon which is readily accessible for cleaning. To remove the nylon filter (*see* Fig. 15) unscrew the banjo bolt (22), remove the steeel washer, the banjo (23), and then the nylon filter (24).

To remove the main jet (13), remove the main-jet cover nut (12) and unscrew the jet from the jet holder (14). Remove the jet block locating-screw (39) to the left of and slightly below the pilot air-adjusting screw (29). Then push or tap out the jet block (16) through the larger end of the mixing chamber body. To remove the pilot jet (9), remove the pilot-jet cover nut (11) and unscrew the jet.

Cleaning the Carburettor. Wash all the carburettor components thoroughly clean with petrol and blow through the various ducts and passages to ensure that they are quite clear. Do not use a fluffy rag for drying purposes. Pay special attention to the small pilot jet passages in the jetblock. Be sure to remove all impurities from the inside of the float chamber. Also do not forget to clean the detachable pilot jet and the nylon filter shown at (24) in Fig. 15.

Inspecting the Components. If the carburettor had been in continuous service for a considerable period inspect the various components after dismantling the carburettor. Note the following.

1. *The Float Chamber.* Check that the vent is unobstructed and that the float is in perfect condition. Clean the moulded-nylon needle very thoroughly, and be careful not to damage it. If it tends to stick in its seating, relieve its three bearing edges with a fine file. The needle seating shown at (25) in Fig. 15 must be absolutely clean. See that the small nylon filter (24) is undamaged and contains no obstructions. Check that the joint faces of the float-chamber cover and the float chamber are not damaged or bruised, and that the joint washer is in sound condition, otherwise some petrol leakage from the cover joint may occur.

2. *The Throttle Valve.* Check that the throttle valve slides in the mixing chamber without excessive play. If excessive play exists, renew the throttle valve immediately.

3. *The Jet-needle Clip.* The spring clip securing the tapered jet-needle to the throttle valve must grip the needle firmly, and free rotation of the needle must occur, otherwise the needle groove will will become worn and necessitate a new needle being fitted. When the carburettor is reassembled be sure to replace the jet-needle with the spring clip in the correct needle groove (*see* page 39).

4. *The Needle-jet.* Inspect its orifice for signs of wear which are generally present after a mileage of about 15,000 miles. The tapered jet-needle is made of hard stainless-steel and its tapered part does not wear.

5. *The Jet Block.* Before tapping this home in the mixing chamber verify by blowing that the pilot-jet ducts are unobstructed and see that the jet block fibre seal (shown at (40) in Fig. 14) is in good condition.

6. *The Carburettor Flange.* Examine this for truth with a straight-edge. Slight distortion sometimes occurs after a considerable mileage, and this may cause an air leak. See that the heat-resisting joint washer is in perfect condition. If it is not, renew it. If the face of the carburettor flange is slightly concave, file the face carefully and then rub the face on emery cloth laid on a surface plate until a straight-edge shows the face surface to be dead flat. Alternatively have the face machined dead flat by using a grinder at a service garage.

To Reassemble "Monobloc" Carburettor. Assemble the carburettor in the reverse order of dismantling. Referring to Fig. 14, screw home the pilot jet (9) and the pilot-jet cover nut (11), not omitting to replace its washer. Push or tap home the jet block (16) and fibre seal (40) through the large end of the mixing chamber (3). Check that the fibre seal fitted to the stub of the jet block is in sound condition. Then fit the jet block locating-screw (39). Screw the main-jet holder (14) into the jet block after checking that the washer for the holder is sound and that the needle-jet (15) is securely screwed into the top of the holder. Now screw home the main jet (13) into the base of the main-jet holder and replace the main-jet cover nut (12).

Fig. 15. Showing the nylon filter and adjacent parts

For key to numbered parts, see page 35
(The Enfield Cycle Co. Ltd.)

Replace the moulded-nylon needle (26) in the float chamber (37), and fit the hinged float (27) with the *narrow* side of the hinge uppermost. It must contact the nylon needle. Do not omit the short distance collar on the spindle. Afterwards fit the float-chamber cover (38) and replace the three securing screws (28). Be careful to tighten these three screws evenly. Before replacing the cover it is advisable to renew the washer and make sure that the float chamber and cover joint faces are absolutely clean. Replace items (22)–(24) shown in Fig. 15. Note that the small nylon filter (24) has longitudinal supports moulded in its sides. When replacing the filter see that these supports do not obstruct the feed holes in (25), otherwise some petrol starvation may result. Tighten the banjo bolt (22) securely when the petrol pipe is later connected to the banjo by the union nut.

If previously removed, attach the jet-needle (6) to the throttle valve (5) and secure with the jet-needle clip (4) (*see* Fig 14). Make sure that the clip enters the correct groove on the needle (*see* page 39).

Fit the heat-resisting washer to the face on the cylinder barrel. Renew it if not in perfect condition. Some models have a rubber "O" ring. Then smear a little oil on the outside of the throttle valve and ease the throttle valve (5) and the air valve (17), where fitted, down into the mixing chamber (3). When easing the throttle valve home make sure that the tapered jet-needle (6) really enters the hole in the jet block (16). Offer up the carburettor and secure its flange firmly to the cylinder barrel face and washer by means of the two nuts. It is important to tighten both nuts the same amount. Tighten down firmly the mixing-chamber knurled lock ring (2) so as to secure the mixing-chamber cap (1), and see that the throttle valve slides up and down freely when the cap is secured. Finally re-connect the petrol pipe and firmly tighten the union nut and the banjo bolt shown at (22) in Fig. 15.

The Correct Amal Carburettor (Settings 1958–66). All new 1958–66 Model D5, D7, D7D/L Bantam motor-cycles have the carburettor settings given below and the makers recommend that these settings should not be altered.

Main jet: 140.
Pilot jet: 25
Throttle valve: 375/3½.
Needle position: 2
Needle-jet: 0·1055.

CONCENTRIC CARBURETTOR DETAILS (1967–70)

This carburettor is a development of the "Monobloc" carburettor, dealt with in the previous pages, and the principles of operation, tuning, etc., are the same for both instruments. It is only the constructional details which differ, as will be seen by comparing Fig. 14 (Monobloc carburettor) with Fig. 16 (Concentric carburettor). It should be noted that the air slide, which is controlled by a spring-loaded plunger (Fig. 2) on the standard carburettor, is coupled by cable to a lever on the right handlebar for the Concentric carburettor. The latter is also fitted with a rubber sealing ring at the joint face with the cylinder barrel, to ensure an airtight connection. As already mentioned, most of the information provided for the Monobloc carburettor is suitable for both types, any essential differences being explained in the following notes.

The Pilot Air-adjusting Screw and the Throttle Stop. These are fitted with a rubber "O" ring, (a) to retain the screw adjustment, and (b) to prevent air leaks.

The Main Jet. This becomes accessible after the float chamber has been removed (retained by two screws). Reference to Fig. 16 shows that the main jet screws into the jet holder, which in turn screws into the carburettor body. On very late Bantam 175 models the float-chamber body incorporates a hollow drain plug which should be removed periodically and any sediment cleaned out. The aperture may also be used as an access point

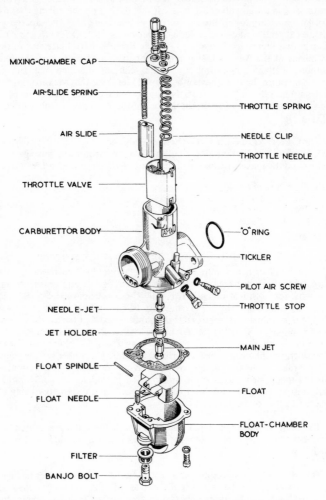

MIXING-CHAMBER CAP

AIR-SLIDE SPRING

THROTTLE SPRING

AIR SLIDE

NEEDLE CLIP

THROTTLE NEEDLE

THROTTLE VALVE

CARBURETTOR BODY

"O" RING

TICKLER

PILOT AIR SCREW

THROTTLE STOP

NEEDLE-JET

JET HOLDER

MAIN JET

FLOAT SPINDLE

FLOAT

FLOAT NEEDLE

FLOAT-CHAMBER BODY

FILTER

BANJO BOLT

Fig. 16. Exploded view of Amal "Concentric" carburettor

for removal of the main jet. When this is replaced do not screw in too tightly, otherwise when unscrewing at a future date the jet holder may also be unscrewed.

The Jet-needle and Needle Jet. The notes given for the Monobloc carburettor apply here, except that the jet needle has four grooves only.

The Pilot Jet. As with the main jet, the pilot jet is accessible after removal of the float chamber and screws into the underside of the carburettor body (Fig. 16). It should be noted that, on most D14 and all Bantam 175 models, this jet is not detachable and in fact is not even visible (*see below*).

MAINTENANCE (CONCENTRIC CARBURETTOR)

Altering Slow-runnning Adjustment. The notes given for the Monobloc carburettor apply in this instance, except that the air slide is *opened* by means of the handlebar lever, which must be turned in a *clockwise* direction as far as possible.

To Clear an Obstructed Pilot Jet. Unscrew the pilot jet and clean as described on page 35. On most D14 and all Bantam 175 models, where this jet is not detachable, it must be cleared by the use of compressed air applied to the outer hole on the face of the carburettor intake. It will, of course, be necessary to disconnect the flexible pipe from the air cleaner, to expose this, and other, holes.

Dismantling the Concentric Carburettor. Turn off the petrol and unscrew the banjo bolt beneath the float chamber, thus releasing the petrol-pipe connection and also the smaller filter. Remove both nuts from the carburettor flange and draw the carburettor off its studs. Watch for the "O" ring inserted in the joint face.

Take off the carburettor top cover (using the correct type of screwdriver!), complete with the air-slide and throttle-valve assemblies. To remove the needle from the throttle slide, first compress the spring and then extract the needle clip. With the spring still compressed, the cable nipple can be released from the throttle valve. A similar procedure allows the cable to be released from the air slide.

Next, take off the float-chamber body, which is attached to the carburettor body by two screws, and take care not to damage the gasket during this operation. The float can then be lifted out of the chamber, and it should be noted at this stage that the needle groove fits into the forked tongue on the float and that the spindle is a tight fit in the float chamber slots.

If further dismantling is required, unscrew the main jet and then the jet holder from the base of the carburettor body. On many of the Concentric carburettors fitted to Bantam engines, the pilot jet can also be unscrewed, although on the later models the jet is not detachable and is fixed in position within the main body of the carburettor.

If required, the throttle stop and the pilot air screw may be taken out, in which case take good care of their "O" rings. The primer (or "tickler") may also be removed, but since this item is not in frequent use it is not likely to be worn sufficiently to require replacement.

Cleaning the Carburettor. See notes on page 37.

Inspecting the Carburettor. *See* notes for Monobloc carburettor, page 37. It will be noticed by comparison of Figs. 14 and 16 that the Concentric carburettor is not fitted with a "jet block."

Reassembling the Concentric Carburettor. Reassembly does not present any difficulties if Fig. 16 is carefully studied, but one or two points may require further comment.

Firstly, before assembly, all components must be absolutely clean and free from any foreign matter. The gasket between the float chamber and the carburettor must be in good order and if there is any doubt about this, renew the gasket. Similar remarks apply to the "O" rings fitted to the throttle stop and pilot air screws.

If possible use a torque spanner set to 120 lb in. to tighten the jet holder in position, while a torque of 50 lb in. is required for the main jet.

When the float and needle has been reassembled, check that the rise and fall of the float causes a corresponding movement of the needle. If there is any sign of wear on the tapered seat of the needle, a new one should be fitted, otherwise the petrol level will be affected.

Carburettor Settings (1967–70). The settings for the D10 and D14 Bantam engines are given below. Do not alter any of these items.

1967: D10	Main jet 150, pilot 25, throttle valve 3, needle position 2, needle jet 0·105
1968: D14	Main jet 160, pilot 25, throttle valve 3, needle position 3, needle jet 0·105
1969–70: D14 and Bantam 175	Main jet 180, pilot 622/107, throttle 3½, needle position 2, needle jet 0·105

4 Maintaining a good spark

By keeping the ignition system at maximum efficiency you will be assured of a "fat" spark occurring regularly at the sparking plug. This ensures rapid starting-up under all weather conditions, and guarantees complete and quick combustion of fuel in the combustion chamber, factors vital to good performance and minimum fuel consumption.

Six Bantam Ignition/Lighting Systems. On all 1948–66 Bantams an efficient flywheeel generator (which incorporates the contact-breaker) is provided for supplying the current required for ignition and lighting. For the years 1967–70 the flywheel type of generator was discontinued in favour of separate generator and contact-breaker units, the former being mounted on the left side of the crankshaft and the latter on the right side of the crankshaft within a special oil-tight housing, comprising part of the primary chaincase. This chapter, apart from a general introductory paragraph, deals only with those components concerned with ignition, the components of the lighting system being dealt with in detail in the next chapter. The ignition and lighting systems, although dealt with in separate chapters, cannot be regarded as independent systems. Below is a brief outline of the six ignition/lighting systems used on 1948–70 B.S.A. Bantams.

The 1948–50 direct ignition and lighting system (Model D1) where a Wipac (Wico-Pacy) a.c. flywheel "Geni-mag" supplies a.c. current direct to the sparking plug and a.c. current direct to the headlamp main bulb. A bicycle-type *dry* battery incorporated inside the headlamp supplies current for illuminating the pilot bulb and tail lamp.

2. *The 1951–65 direct ignition and lighting system* (Models D1, D3, D5, D7) where a Wipac a.c./d.c. flywheel generator (type S55/Mk. 8) supplies d.c. current direct to the sparking plug, and a.c. current direct to the headlamp main bulb. A bicycle-type *dry* battery inside the headlamp lights the pilot bulb and tail lamp.

3. *The 1950–3 coil-ignition and battery lighting system* (Model D1) where a Lucas a.c. flywheel generator (type 1A45) supplies current via a rectifier to a Lucas lead-acid battery from which d.c. current is drawn for coil ignition and illuminating *all* lamps.

4. *The 1954–64 battery lighting system* (Models D1, D3 and D5) where a Wipac a.c./d.c. flywheel generator (type S55/Mk. 8) feeds d.c. current to the

sparking plug and d.c. current via a rectifier to a Varley or Lucas lead-acid battery from which current is drawn for lighting *all* lamps.

5. *The 1964–6 coil ignition and battery lighting system* (Models D7, D7D/L) where a Wipac a.c./d.c. generator (type S55/Mk. 8) supplies a.c. current direct to the headlamp main bulb and trickle-charges d.c. current to a Lucas lead-acid battery responsible for coil ignition and lighting the headlamp pilot bulb and stop–tail lamp.

6. *The 1967–70 coil ignition and battery lighting system* (Models D10 and D14) where a Wipac alternator supplies current via a rectifier to the battery, the charge rate varying with the lighting switch positions. The battery is used as the source of all the electrical requirements, including coil ignition and head and parking lights. The system also accommodates a method for emergency starting with a discharged battery, when the lights must be extinguished and the ignition switch moved to a special position, thus diverting full generator (alternator) output to the battery. *This switch position must not be used for more than a quarter of an hour, because of the very high charging rate involved.*

NOTE: where system (1), (2) or (5) is utilized the headlamp main bulb cannot be illuminated *unless the engine is running*. On all Bantams the electric horn is operated by current from the dry battery or lead-acid battery according to which type is fitted.

THE SPARKING PLUG

On a two-stroke engine the sparking plug fires once every engine revolution and, as might be expected, the combusion chamber is an extremely hot place. It is therefore essential always to run on a reputable make of plug of the correct type.

Suitable Plugs for Bantams. All 1948 and subsequent Bantams require a 14 mm sparking plug with a 12·5 mm ($\frac{1}{2}$ in.) reach except for the years 1967–70 when "long-reach" plugs were fitted ($\frac{3}{4}$ in). Three excellent makes of sparking plug are the Champion, the Lodge, and the K.L.G. Any of these plugs can be relied upon to give satisfactory results. N.G.K. plugs are also suitable.

B.S.A. Motor Cycles Ltd. have always fitted as official factory equipment Champion sparking plugs which in their opinion are well suited to the particular requirements of the B.S.A. power units.

CHAMPION. Always fit a single-point, non-detachable type L–10 to 1948–53 Bantams (cast-iron heads). On 1954–66 Models D1, D3, D5, D7 and D7D/L (alloy heads) fit a type L–7. For 1967–70 Models D10, D14, and Bantam 175, use type N4.

LODGE. Fit type CN on 1948–54 Model D1 Bantams (cast-iron heads), and an HN plug on 1955–66 Model 5 D1, D3, D5, D7 and D7D/L Bantams (light-alloy heads) For 1967–70 Models D10, D14, Bantam 175, fit type HLN.

K.L.G. Always fit a type F75 on 1955–66 models, but for all subsequent years (i.e. 1967–70) use FE75.

On 1948–54 models (cast-iron heads) fit an F50 plug.

Weatherproof Plug Terminal Covers. All-weather Bantam riders would do well to consider fitting a weatherproof plug terminal cover or (if the old plug requires to be renewed) a watertight plug. Excellent Champion, Lodge, and K.L.G. waterproof terminal covers are available which give complete plug protection by thorough shielding of the top insulation, and prevent the risk of a short circuit being caused by water, dirt, or oil getting on the insulator. They are quickly-detachable and will fit any standard type of plug, assuming that the covers and plugs are of the same make.

Symptoms of Faulty Plug. If no spark occurs between the plug electrodes, the engine will fail to start up, or if the engine has been running, will suddenly stop. Should the plug fire, but intermittently, the symptoms will be difficulty in starting up, misfiring, with perhaps some banging in the silencer, and erratic slow-running. All these symptoms are most annoying. If the plug is suspected to be faulty, test it immediately.

How to Test a Plug. The accepted and quite satisfactory method of testing a sparking plug for good sparking is to lay it on the cylinder head or other convenient metal part with the terminal (if unprotected by a moulded terminal cover) clear of the head; then smartly rotate the engine by means of the kick-starter and observe whether the plug sparks regularly and well. A spark should occur at every engine revolution. It should be distinctly visible in daylight, and it should be possible to hear a distinct "click" as the spark bridges the gap between the electrodes.

If only a weak spark occurs in spite of a good spark being obtainable at the end of the h.t. lead thoroughly inspect the sparking plug and, if still usable, service it.

Inspect the Sparking Plug Every 1,000 Miles. Remove the plug about every 1,000 miles for careful inspection. On a new engine inspect the plug after the first 500 miles. If the Amal carburettor is correctly tuned, the electrodes should remain clean for a long period. A rich mixture, however, will soon cause the points to acquire a sooty deposit, and this deposit will also adhere to the base of the plug before long. Note that a wrongly pro-portioned petroil mixture (*see* page 17) will result in fouling of the plug. Leaded fuels are also apt to cause grey-coloured deposits.

Before deciding that a sparking plug is no longer serviceable, examine it very closely. If inspection reveals that the electrodes are badly burned, put the plug in the nearest dustbin, not in the cylinder head. Where bad burning occurs within a short period, this indicates an incorrect mixture or too small a plug gap.

Light-coloured fuel deposits affect efficiency to a very small extent, except when accompanied by a bad condition of the plug or oiling-up. Nevertheless they should always be removed completely. Look for soft or hard carbon deposits which affect efficiency considerably, and especially when they collect inside the plug body. Such deposits can cause internal sparking and spoil engine performance, or even cause a complete stoppage. All carbon deposits must be completely removed by thoroughly cleaning the plug.

Carbon deposits are caused by mixture fouling, and by oil fouling. In the former instance the deposits are dull black and sooty, but in the latter case they are generally shiny black, hard, and moist. Should rapid fouling take place, you can often diagnose the origin of the trouble by carefully noting the precise nature of the deposits.

Oiling-up. Inspect for oiling-up which sometimes occurs together with the presence of carbon deposits. An oiled-up plug is generally dirty and wet with oil. Careful cleaning is called for. During the first 1,000 miles, i.e. when running-in the engine, there is sometimes a tendency for oiling-up to occur, but this tendency should gradually disappear. If oiling-up occurs after running-in, this is caused through using an incorrect petroil mixture, poorly fitted or worn piston rings, or a worn cylinder barrel and/or piston skirt.

Insulation of Plug. Check during the inspection of the plug that the insulation has not become damaged or cracked, and that it is externally clean.

Do Not Forget the Plug Washer. See that the washer located between the cylinder head and plug body is not damaged. Renew this washer if it has become badly flattened and hard (thereby reducing conductivity of heat); also renew it if its condition is likely to cause loss of compression or "blowing."

On Champion plugs, the washer is an integral part, and will last for the life of the plug.

Check the Plug Gap. When removing the sparking plug for inspection and cleaning, always check the gap between the electrodes (points). B.S.A. Motor Cycles Ltd. recommend a gap for all plugs of between 0·020 in. and 0·025 in. when used with coil-ignition systems or 0·018 in. with "direct" ignition. Difficult starting up, misfiring, and an indifferent engine performance are sometimes caused by an incorrect gap. An excessive gap tends to overheat the centre electrode and cause pre-ignition, while an insufficient gap obviously increases any latent tendency for oiling-up to occur.

The gap slowly but surely increases and it is therefore advisable about every 1,000 miles (when inspecting the sparking plug) to check the plug gap with a suitable feeler gauge which can be obtained from any large accessory firm.

After making sure that the plug points are quite clean, insert the appropriate blade of the feeler gauge between the earthed (outer) electrode(s) and the insulated (centre) electrode. Should you find that the plug gap is outside the limits 0·020–0·025 in., you should re-gap the plug immediately. An excellent tool for checking the gap and regapping the plug is the combined Champion regapping tool and feeler gauge. This is an inexpensive tool which is suited for any make of plug.

To Regap the Sparking Plug. An adjustment to correct the gap should always be made by bending the *earth* (outer) electrode(s). Never attempt to move the insulated (centre) electrode, or you will ruin the plug. Do not tap the electrode(s), but gently *press* towards the centre electrode, using the Champion tool as shown in Fig. 17; the tool is obtainable from any

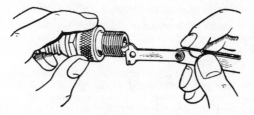

Fig. 17. Regapping sparking plug with Champion tool

The Champion tool shown includes suitable gauges

Champion plug stockist or from the plug makers. Continue to make an adjustment until the correct gap is obtained. Obviously, when regapping a plug it is best to adjust the points to the lower limit (0·020 in.) as the plug will then not require further regapping for a considerable period.

Cleaning the Plug Quickly. If an inspection of the sparking plug shows that it is not badly fouled, it is generally sufficient to brighten up the electrode points with some *fine* glass-paper, or to scrape them clean with the blade of a small pen-knife. Clean the outside of the plug with a cloth moistened with paraffin or petrol.

Note that the plugs recommended for Bantam engines are of the non-detachable type and cannot be dismantled for thorough cleaning.

To Clean Plugs Thoroughly. Visit a garage with an abrasive blast service unit installed. Within a few minutes the plug will then be automatically scoured of all deposits, washed, subjected to a high-pressure air line, and finally tested for good sparking at a pressure in excess of 100 lb per sq in. Renew the plug if it fails to pass this test satisfactorily. Any type of sparking plug can be cleaned and tested in this manner.

If no "air blast" service unit is conveniently available, remove the plug from the cylinder head, pour a little petrol down between the insulated central electrode and the plug body, and set fire to the plug.

Before screwing the plug back into the cylinder head, wipe the tip and outside of the insulation absolutely clean, and polish the electrode points with some *fine* glass-paper. Finally check the gap between the points (0·020–0·025 in.).

Replacing the Plug. Before screwing the plug into the cylinder head, clean the external threads (carbon is a poor conductor) with a wire brush, and check that the washer is in good condition (*see* page 46). Use only normal hand pressure on the plug spanner, and verify that the h.t. lead or terminal cover is firmly secured to the plug terminal.

THE WIPAC FLYWHEEL GENERATORS

On 1948–50 Model D1 Bantams (up to engine No. YDI–40660) provided with Wipac (Wico-Pacy) flywheel generators giving ignition and lighting, the equipment specified includes the Wipac 27-watt "Geni-mag" ignition and a.c. lighting unit.

On 1951–66 Models D1 (after engine No. YDI–40660), D3, D7, D5 with Wipac flywheel generators giving direct ignition and lighting, direct ignition and battery lighting, or coil-ignition and battery lighting, the equipment used includes the Wipac flywheel a.c./d.c. series S55/Mk. 8 generator.

Both the above types of flywheel generator comprise two assemblies: (a) the flywheel, and (b) the stator which carries the ignition coil, the lighting coils, the contact-breaker unit, and condenser. Ignition, except on models with coil-ignition and battery lighting, is direct from the flywheel generator, a desirable characteristic of which is its constant spark output over a wide timing range. The necessity for frequent contact-breaker adjustment is thereby avoided. The contact-breaker and other parts are, however, extremely accessible, and such maintenance as is required is simply effected.

On 1967–70 models D10, D14, and Bantam 175, the generator and contact-breaker are separate entities, situated at opposite ends of the crankshaft, the contact-breaker being housed within a separate compartment (cast integrally with the primary chaincase) and accessible after removal of the large cover. A special seal is used to keep the compartment free from oil contamination. The generator (in this case known as an alternator) is exposed when the left-side crankcase cover is removed and since there is an air gap between the rotor (rotating central portion) and the stator (fixed outer portion) wear cannot take place between these components and hence maintenance is unnecessary.

Check Contact-breaker Adjustment Every 5,000 Miles. About every 5,000 miles carefully check the gap between the contact-breaker points (studs with very hard metal faces ground flat). Remove the contact-breaker cover, secured by a spring clip or two fixing screws (August, 1949, onwards). Then turn the engine over slowly until the contacts are wide apart; slip a suitable feeler gauge between them. The correct gap is 0·015 in. (0·38 mm). If the gap varies appreciably from the specified gap, make a contact-breaker adjustment as described below.

Referring to Figs. 18, 19, and 20, with a small screwdriver slacken off the locking screw E above the contacts about one turn. Then in the case of the "Geni-mag" contact-breaker (1948–50) turn the eccentric adjuster-screw F (Fig. 18) clockwise or anti-clockwise as required until the contact-breaker gap is found to be correct. In the case of the Wipac a.c./d.c. series S55/Mk. 8 ignition/lighting generator (1951–66), after loosening the screw E (Figs. 19, 20), move the fixed contact plate[1] (with a suitable screwdriver engaged in the recess provided) up or down until the 0·015 in. blade of the feeler gauge just enters the gap without binding. Afterwards firmly retighten the locking screw E.

Referring to Fig. 21 for the 1967–70 models, slacken the locking screw E, rotate the eccentric pin H until the gap between the points is 0·012 in., and retighten screw E.

Cleaning the Contacts. Occasionally clean the contacts of the contact-breaker by inserting a smooth piece of cloth or paper between them and withdrawing the paper while the contacts are in the closed position. Always keep the contacts absolutely clean and free from oil, grease, and petrol, otherwise they will become blackened, burned, and perhaps pitted. If the contacts are discoloured or slightly pitted, polish them lightly with a small piece of smooth fine-grade emery cloth. Avoid rubbing the contacts excessively. When the contacts are closed, they must be tight and in line.

Renewing the Contacts. Note that the moving contact is integral with the contact-breaker rocker arm. Should either contact be in such a condition as to require renewal, see that the other contact is renewed simultaneously. The renewal of contacts individually is not practicable.

When assembling the moulded rocker arm, prime the pivot pin lightly with some oil or soft grease. The rocker arm on the "Geni-mag" is of the self-lubricating type, but on the later models (1951–70) it is beneficial to prime the pivot pin at occasional and regular intervals. When replacing the rocker arm, be careful to insert the correct number of thin spacing washers behind the rocker arm so as to align the contacts truly and to ensure proper insulation. Then anchor the end of the contact-breaker spring to the terminal post with the screw and shake-proof washer. Position one of the spring washers over the pivot on the outer side of the rocker arm and insert the spring clip in the groove or, in the case of the 1967–70 models, tighten the screw.

---

[1] On no account ever attempt to bend the fixed-contact plate.

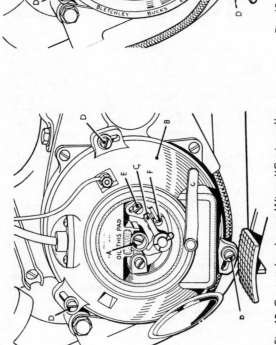

Fig. 19. Contact-breaker on Wipac S55/Mk. 8 generator (1951–63)

Applicable to Wipac direct ignition and lighting models, also Wipac battery-lighting models

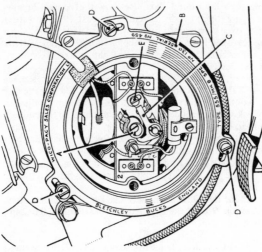

Fig. 18. Contact-breaker on Wipac "Geni-mag" (1948–50)

Applicable to direct ignition and lighting models

Key to Figs. 18, 19, 20

A. Contact-breaker cam
B. Contact-breaker housing
C. Rocker arm
D. Screw securing B
E. Screw securing fixed contact
F. Eccentric adjuster screw

Wear of Rocker-arm Heel. When a flywheel generator (or contact-breaker unit on later models) has been in use for very many thousands of miles, some wear may occur on the rocker-arm heel. This is liable to cause loss of power and irregular running. If such symptoms develop and the rocker arm is suspect, inspect the heel and carefully scrutinize its edges which bear against the cam. If the heel is in good condition, the edges should be sharply defined. If they are rounded, considerable wear has obviously occurred, and the rocker arm must be renewed.

A Weak Condenser. If the condenser becomes weak, sparking occurs across the contacts of the contact-breaker, accompanied by burning of the contacts. An intense blue spark is a definite indication of a weak condenser whose function is to prevent excessive build-up of l.t. current. A weak condenser should be renewed immediately.

Wipac Generator Timing. This is accurately set to very close limits by the makers, and no ignition advance and retard lever is included on the handle-bars because in practice manual control has been found to be entirely unnecessary. On all Wipac "Geni-mags" and Wipac a.c./d.c. flywheel generators the contact-breaker cam (shown at *A* in Figs. 18, 19, 20) is keyed to an extension of the flywheel main-shaft, and it is therefore obvious that its position relative to that of the piston is absolutely fixed (only one key is provided).

As may be seen in Figs. 18, 19, 20, the contact-breaker housing *B* has slotted lugs for the three housing-securing screws, and this enables a limited variation in the ignition timing to be made where required. After slackening the three securing screws *D*, the contact-breaker housing *B* can be rotated through a small angle. Afterwards the three securing screws must be firmly retightened.

From Fig. 21 it will be seen that the contact-breaker back plate *B* is slotted to accept the fixing screws *D*. When these are slackened the plate can be moved through a very limited arc.

Provided that the ignition timing has not been disturbed, it should *never* be necessary for the private owner to make an ignition timing adjustment. Experimental variation of the timing must *not* be made. The small adjustment provided is to facilitate the accurate setting of the ignition timing at the Bantam factory and is not designed for the use of "Bantamites." Note that the change over to premium grade fuels does not permit of an advance in the ignition timing where Bantams are concerned. Also note that to ensure correct ignition timing, as well as proper electrical functioning of the magneto portion of the flywheel generator, it is essential to maintain the correct gap between the contacts (wide open) of the contact-breaker (*see* page 49).

To Check Ignition Timing. Should you have good reason to doubt the accuracy of the ignition timing, you can readily check it. First verify that

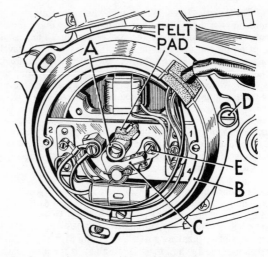

Fig. 20. Contact-breaker on Wipac S55/Mk. 8 generator (1964–6)

Applicable to all coil-ignition and battery lighting models. This also applies, except as regards the wiring layout, to all 1964–5 models with a direct ignition and lighting system

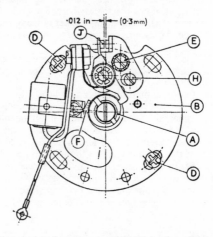

Fig. 21. Contact-breaker unit on 1967–70 models (D10, D14, and Bantam 175)

the contact-breaker gap is correct (*see* page 49). Next remove the sparking plug and rotate the engine slowly until the piston is exactly at top dead centre (T.D.C.). To find the true T.D.C. position, insert a suitable rod through the plug hole and "rock" the engine slowly with the piston right up. When the "rock" produces no piston movement, the piston is exactly at T.D.C. Now turn the engine back until the piston has descended $\frac{5}{32}$ in. ($\frac{1}{16}$ in., D5 and D7; 0·076 in., D10 and 0·057 in. for D14 and Bantam 175). Scratch a mark on the rod to indicate the precise descent of the piston, or alternatively remove the cylinder head and measure the piston descent with a steel rule. When the piston has been correctly positioned, the contact-breaker rocker arm should be just beginning to rise on the contact-breaker cam, and the contacts should have opened not more than 0·002 in. (0·05 mm). A larger opening indicates that the ignition is excessively advanced, whereas a smaller opening indicates that the ignition is excessively retarded. A small variation in the timing, however, will not adversely affect engine performance.

Removing Condenser (1948–50 "Geni-mag"). Should the condenser fail (causing rapid burning of the contacts), renew it immediately. To remove a faulty condenser, first detach the stator by unscrewing the three clamp nuts. You can then gently ease the stator off the three stator-plate studs. Be careful when doing this not to bend it, or you may break the lead connecting the lighting coils to the terminal on the stator. Now disconnect the lead from the terminal post and unscrew the clamp nut located on the securing-spring post of the contact-breaker cover.

When fitting a new condenser, see that its lead is pushed down as far as possible into the well formed by the stator housing otherwise the flywheel may rub, and possibly sever, the lead.[1] The flywheel rim also reaches to within about $\frac{1}{16}$ in. of the head of the insulated lighting-terminal stud, and this must be kept pushed down below this level.

Removing Condenser (1951–66 Wipac Generators). As may be seen in Figs. 19, 20, the condenser is extremely accessible. To withdraw it, remove the condenser-terminal nut and free the condenser lead. Then uncrew the condenser bracket fixing-screw and lift the condenser away. Observe the note at the foot of this page.[1]

Removing Condenser (1967–70 Wipac Contact-breakers). The screw securing the condenser bracket is located below the felt lubricating pad, which will also be released as the screw is withdrawn. Disconnect the condenser earth-lead at the screw which serves the purpose of retaining the moving contact spring and remove the condenser.

---

[1] It is extremely important that all stray loops of wire are kept bent in to behind the radius of the stator.

To Remove Contact-breaker and Stator Unit (Wipac S55/Mk. 8 Generator).
Referring to Figs. 19, 20 remove the cover plate from the contact-breaker
after removing the two-securing screws. Next remove the central screw
securing cam *A* and pull the cam away; lift out the key which locates it on
its shaft. Then remove the three screws *D* holding the contact-breaker
housing, and lift off the housing, complete with contact-breaker and stator
unit.

Important Warning (1948–66 Wipac Generators). In the case of "Geni-
mags" and the later Wipac a.c./d.c. flywheel lighting-ignition generators
it is extremely important to note that *under no circumstances should you
attempt to remove either the generator flywheel or generator rotor from the
engine near-side main shaft without using the special B.S.A. extractors
supplied for the purpose.* If you attempt removal without using these extractors, you will almost certainly cause serious damage to the main
shaft. It is advisable to entrust this type of work to a Bantam repair specialist or any competent dealer.

1967–70 Wipac Generators. The rotor is mounted on a parallel shaft and
keyed in position. An extractor is not necessary for removal.

Flywheels Are Not Interchangeable. Note that the series S55/Mk. 8 a.c./
d.c. ignition generator has more magnets in the flywheel than the 27-watt
"Geni-mag" which is purely an a.c. unit. The two flywheels, although of
similar appearance, are therefore not interchangeable.
    The S55/Mk. 8 flywheel can be readily identified as it is clearly marked
"WIPAC AC/DC." It is also essential that the correct stator plate is used
in conjunction with the appropriate flywheel, otherwise trouble will occur.

Servicing Wipac Generators. Unless you happen to be an electrical
expert (in which case refer to B.S.A. Service Sheets Nos. 810, 810A), you
are not advised to tackle any servicing of "Gemi-mags" (1948–50) or S55/
Mk. 8 ignition lighting generators (1951 onwards) other than normal
maintenance, i.e. the lubrication (page 20), cleaning and adjustment of the
contact-breaker, and the renewal where necessary of the contacts and the
condenser.
    Should the ignition coils, stator, flywheel rotor, etc., develop trouble
and need any attention, ride or deliver the *complete machine* to the nearest
authorized Wico-Pacy service station where the equipment will receive
expert attention. The appropriate address can be obtained from Wipac
Group Sales Ltd., Buckingham, Bucks.

LUCAS COIL-IGNITION

On many 1950–3 123 c.c. Model D1 Bantams, Lucas coil-ignition equipment (first fitted, December, 1949) is provided as an alternative to the

Wipac "Geni-mag" or a.c./d.c. S55/Mk. 8 flywheel generator, dealt with in previous sections.

The Lucas equipment differs fundamentally from the Wipac direct ignition (and lighting) equipment in that a 45-watt Lucas a.c. flywheel generator (type 1A45) supplies current to a 5 amp-hr Lucas type LVW5E lead-acid battery, a rectifier being incorporated to convert a.c. to d.c. for battery charging. Current stored in the battery is then drawn upon for lighting purposes and the coil-ignition system, which, of course, includes an ignition coil, a cam-operated contact-breaker (on the generator), and an ignition switch in the centre of the headlamp rotary-type lighting switch.

The Lucas a.c. Generator. Some details of the a.c. generator and notes concerning its output are given on page 61. Except so far as the contact-breaker is concerned, no maintenance is necessary.

Use of Ignition Switch. The EMG, OFF, and IGN positions of the three-way ignition switch in the centre of the lighting switch on the SSP575P Lucas headlamp are fully explained on page 6, and the correct use of the ignition switch is made clear from these instructions. The following important point concerning the ignition switch is emphasized.

Never attempt to start up your Bantam with the battery disconnected from the circuit and the ignition switch in either the IGN or EMG position. (*See* page 10.)

Servicing a.c. Generator. Except in the event of your being a genuine electrical expert (in which case refer to B.S.A. Service Sheets Nos. 812 and 812A) it is not advisable to undertake any servicing of the Lucas 1A45 generator (1950–3) other than normal maintenance, namely, the lubrication (page 20), cleaning, and adjustment of the contact-breaker, and the renewal, if required, of the contact points and the condenser.

In the event of the stator coils, stator, rotor, etc., developing a fault, send or ride the complete machine to the nearest authorized Lucas service station for expert attention. The appropriate address can be obtained from Joseph Lucas (Sales and Service) Ltd., Great Hampton Street, Birmingham, 19. In the London area the largest service station is at Dordrecht Road, Acton Vale, Acton, W.3.

Inspect the Contact-breaker Gap About Every 3,000 Miles. It is necessary occasionally (say about every 2,500–3,000 miles) to withdraw the contact-breaker cover by removing its two securing screws and then check the gap between the contacts. When the contacts require cleaning (*see* page 56), check the gap *after* cleaning. Provided that the contact-breaker is regularly cleaned, actual adjustment of the contacts is rarely necessary.

To check the gap, rotate the engine slowly until the contacts (*B*, Fig. 22) are observed to be wide open, and then insert a suitable feeler gauge (one is attached to the ignition screwdriver in the tool kit) between the contacts.

The correct gap is 0·010–0·012 in. (0·25–0·30 mm). If the gap differs appreciably from the correct gap, regap the points.

Maintain the engine in a position giving maximum opening of the contacts and loosen screws *D* securing the fixed contact plate (*see* Fig. 22). Then alter the position of this plate until the correct contact-breaker gap is obtained. Afterwards firmly retighten the plate-securing screws.

Cleaning the Contacts. Always inspect the contacts when checking the contact-breaker gap. Never permit the contact-breaker, and especially the contacts, to become oily, greasy, or dirty, otherwise they will rapidly become burned and pitted, and serious ignition trouble will probably occur. If cleaning is necessary, this should be effected *before* making a final gap adjustment. The contacts when in good condition should have a grey, frosted appearance, in which case they should not be interfered with.

To facilitate cleaning of the contacts, it is advisable to detach the moving contact and its spring arm (*see* Fig. 22) from its fixing. To do this, loosen the nuts on the terminal post *A* and lift off the spring which is slotted to assist removal. Then lift the rocker arm off its pivot *C*.

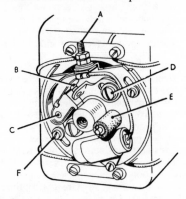

Fig. 22. Contact-breaker on Lucas A.C. generator (1950–3)

Applicable to all models with Lucas coil-ignition and battery lighting

A. Terminal post   D. Screws securing fixed-contact plate
B. Contacts   E. Felt lubricator
C. Rocker-arm pivot   F. Screws securing timing-control plate

If the contacts are not pitted, but merely slightly discoloured, it is generally satisfactory to wipe the contacts with a clean cloth moistened with petrol. But if the contacts are blackened, burned, or pitted, clean them up with a slip of fine carborundum stone, or if not available, some *very fine* emery cloth. During the cleaning and truing up of the contacts, be very careful not to remove more than the barest amount of contact metal to ensure brightness of the surfaces, that the two contacts are parallel, and that the two faces are absolutely smooth. Note that some new Lucas contact sets supplied by Joseph Lucas Ltd. have slightly *convex* faces, and obviously if such contacts are fitted, they should be cleaned only with very fine emery cloth.

After cleaning the contacts, replace the moving contact and spring arm, and check the gap between the contacts as described on page 48. Finally, replace the contact-breaker cover.

Contact-breaker Lubrication. *See* instructions on page 20.

To Remove the Contact-breaker. Remove the contact-breaker-base fixing screws, and then lift up the contact plate, complete with the condenser (*see* Fig. 22). Note the position of the contact-breaker base relative to the generator body and make a suitable mark to avoid the necessity for re-timing the ignition when it is assembled.

The Generator and Rectifier. It is not possible or necessary to make any adjustment to either the Lucas 1A45 generator or CTR1 rectifier.

To remove the generator (not advised except by experts), first remove the cover from the generator and disconnect all wires at the "snap" connectors beneath the forward end of the fuel tank. Next remove the bolt securing the rotor and insert in its place the special rotor extracting-bolt supplied with the machine, and withdraw the rotor until it is just free of the crankshaft. Then remove the nuts and spring washers from the studs passing through the generator body and crankcase, and withdraw the complete generator assembly. On no account remove the rotor from the generator body, or loss of magnetism will result.

Lucas a.c. Generator Timing. The timing ($\frac{5}{32}$ in. before T.D.C.) is accurately set by the makers and should not normally be interfered with; but if desired the timing can readily be checked as described on page 5 for the Wipac flywheel generator. Should it be necessary for some special reason to make a slight variation in the ignition timing, you can do this by slackening off the screws shown at *F* in Fig. 22 and turning the timing control plate a small amount in a clockwise or anti-clockwise direction, according to whether it is desired to advance or retard the spark respectively.

Care of Battery. For instructions on the maintenance of the Lucas lead-acid battery *see* pages 61–4.

The Ignition Coil. The Lucas-type ignition coil (below the fuel tank) must always be kept clean externally, especially between its terminals. The terminal connections must also always be kept tight. Apart from these two points, no maintenance is necessary.

To Remove High Tension Cable. Removal is necessary when the rubber insulation shows signs of perishing or cracking. Always use 7-mm rubber-covered ignition cable for renewal purposes. To connect the cable, thread the knurled moulded nut over the cable, bare the cable end for approximately ¼ in., thread the wire through the metal washer, and bend back the strands. Afterwards screw the nut into its terminal.

5 The lighting equipment

This chapter deals with the lighting components of the flywheel generator, the battery (where rectifier lighting is provided), the headlamp, and the tail lamp or stop–tail lamp. Some useful wiring diagrams are included at the end of the chapter.

Brief reference to various types of Wipac generators fitted to 1948–66 Bantams is made below. See page 61 for details of the Lucas generator on 1950–3 battery-lighting models with coil ignition.

THE FLYWHEEL GENERATOR

The Wipac and Lucas flywheel generators are all of very compact design, and of a type requiring the minimum attention. A few hints concerning their normal maintenance are included in this section.

The Wipac a.c. "Geni-mag" (1948–50 models)

Maintenance. No maintenance is normally required in respect of the magnetic units, lighting, coils, etc. (*See* remarks on page 54 concerning servicing in the event of trouble occurring.) Some ignition components of the flywheel generator do require periodical maintenance, and the appropriate instructions are given on pages 48–54.

The Wipac a.c./d.c. S55/Mk. 8 Generator.

This flywheel generator superseded the "Geni-mag" (August, 1950) which is an a.c. unit. On 1951–65 123 cm³, 148 cm³, 174 cm³ Bantams with Wipac direct ignition and lighting, the permanent-magnet generator produces alternating current direct into the lamp load. On 1954–64 models with Wipac battery-lighting equipment, the generator charges via a rectifier the battery from which current is taken for the lamps and horn.

The generator and rectifier maintain the battery well charged under all running conditions, a system of coil switching varying the generator output according to the prevailing load. The 6-volt a.c./d.c. unit has an output of 30 watts at about 2,800 rev/min. The flywheel comprises six cast magnets with laminated pole pieces. It is "self-keeping," and it is possible to separate the flywheel from the stator without the risk of any loss of magnetism occurring. The laminated stator has six salient poles. Of these, four are wound with coils of enamelled copper wire.

Where a battery is fitted to Model D5 or D7 an a.c./d.c. trickle charge is used. The stator plate has three lighting coils and the two outer coils are connected in series, with one end earthed, to provide a.c. current for the headlamp main bulb. Unless the engine is running the headlamp bulb does not light. The small centre coil is connected via a small full-wave rectifier to the battery and provides trickle charge current with the lighting switch in all positions. The trickle charge system provides battery current to operate the parking lights, stop light and horn.

It is possible for any Bantam owner to convert his a.c. direct lighting set into d.c. (Varley) battery lighting with (Sentercel) rectifier. A suitable Wipac conversion set is obtainable (1948–54). On new 1957–65 B.S.A. Bantams, Wipac direct lighting or battery lighting is specified as alternative equipment. On 1950–3 models, Lucas battery-lighting (*see* page 54) was the alternative equipment.

Maintenance. This is not necessary except in respect of the ignition components, the maintenance of which is dealt with on pages 48–54. Should the generator require any further attention other than the renewal of the contacts and condenser, send or take the complete machine to an authorized Wico-Pacy service station.

Wipac Conversion Kits. It is now possible for any Bantam owner to convert a direct-lighting set into rectifier lighting, with battery. Three types of "Convertakit" kits (requiring no special tools for fitting, and with full instructions) are obtainable from the Wipac Group Sales Ltd., London Road, Buckingham, Bucks., or through B.S.A. agents and accessory dealers. The kits are applicable to 1948–51 Bantams with remote-control lighting switch and to 1952–65 models with built-in rotary-type headlamp switch.

To Remove Wipac Contact-breaker and Stator Unit. First remove the two screws holding the contact-breaker cover plate in position and remove the cover plate. Next remove the central screw securing the cam *A* (*see* Figs. 18, 19 20). Pull the cam away and lift out its key. Now remove the three screws *D* which secure the contact-breaker housing. You can then lift off the whole unit, including the housing.

To Remove Wipac Contact-breaker (Models D10, D14, and Bantam 175, 1967–70). This is simply a matter of removing the two screws *D*, Fig. 21, securing the carrier plate and of uncoupling the earth lead at its snap connector or eyelet. The whole unit may then be withdrawn from its housing.

To Remove the Wipac Flywheel. Never attempt to do this unless you have available the appropriate B.S.A. service tool, namely the flywheel extractor, Part No. 61–3188. Any attempt to remove the flywheel without the extractor will damage the mainshaft.

Before extracting the flywheel, first verify that the cam key has been removed from its key-way. Remove the central nut and its shake-proof washer. Screw the B.S.A. extractor on to the exposed thread as far as it will go. Then with a suitable spanner turn the central extractor bolt until the flywheel is withdrawn from the taper on the mainshaft.

The Lucas a.c. 1A45 Generator. Fitted to many 1950–3 Model D1 Bantams with Lucas battery-lighting and coil ignition, the Lucas a.c. generator is of the inductor type.

When the lamps are switched on, the generator delivers maximum output, and during daylight running with the lighting switch in the OFF position a resistance is inserted into the circuit to reduce the generator output. Turning the headlamp lighting switch to the *H* position (*see* page 9) automatically effects a change-over from reduced to full generator output, the ammeter indicating the amount of current flowing out of or into the battery.

Maintenance. None is necessary except in regard to the ignition contact-breaker (*see* pages 55–7). As regards servicing, *see also* pages 20 and 35. Never attempt to remove the rotor from the stator assembly, otherwise a reduced generator output may ensue, necessitating remagnetizing of the assembly.

BATTERY MAINTENANCE

On Bantams with Lucas coil-ignition and battery-lighting equipment (provided on many 1950–3 models) as an alternative to direct ignition and lighting, the battery feeds current to the headlamp, the tail lamp, the electric horn, and to the ignition coil (except when the ignition switch is in the EMG position). Correct battery maintenance is vital. This section covers the Lucas 5 amp-hr and 9 amp-hr lead-acid batteries (fitted to 1950–3 and 1956–66 battery models respectively) and the Varly 9 amp-hr "dry" battery (used on 1954–5 battery models).

Topping-up a Lucas Battery. It is advisable to inspect the acid level about every *two weeks*, and more frequently in very warm climates. To inspect the level of the electrolyte it is preferable to take the battery right off. Slacken the battery clamping bolt, release the strap, and lift the battery out. On 1956–66 "swinging arm" Bantams unscrew the two nuts under the rear of the dual-seat and lift the latter off to the rear. Then remove the two small bolts securing the battery strap, unscrew the terminals, and withdraw the battery. Now remove the battery lid.

For D10, D14, and Bantam 175 models, it is first necessary to take off the left side panel to expose the battery and then to release the wire clamp retaining the battery to its platform. If the lid is taken off while the battery is still in position, the height of the battery is sufficiently reduced to allow it to be extracted through the aperture in the centre panel.

Unscrew the three filler plugs. Inspect the vent hole in each plug and make sure that it is not choked. See that each rubber washer (where fitted) is undamaged. On no account hold a naked light near the filler-plug holes.

If necessary add distilled water (obtainable from most garages and chemists) as required to bring the electrolyte level up to the top of the separators. *Never use tap water*. Top-up the battery just *before* a daylight run, as the agitation and gassing will mix the solution.

Fig. 23. Topping-up Lucas battery with Lucas battery filler

Before commencing to top-up, wipe the top of the battery clean with a rag to prevent the possibility of any dirt entering the cells. Destroy the rag afterwards as it will corrode any metal parts with which it comes into contact. The most convenient method of topping-up a Lucas battery is to use a Lucas battery filler. Insert the nozzle of the battery filler into each cell as shown in Fig. 23 until the nozzle rests on the separators. Hold the filler in this position until air bubbles cease to rise in the glass container. The cell is then topped-up to the correct level. When all three cells have been topped-up, wipe away all moisture from the top of the battery.

Replenishing the Lucas Battery Filler. When replenishing the Lucas battery filler with distilled water, see that the screw-on nozzle is correctly replaced. Be sure that the rubber washer is fitted over the valve with the small peg in the centre of the valve engaging the hole in the projecting boss of the washer.

Checking the Lucas Battery Condition. Occasionally it is advisable to check the condition of the battery by taking hydrometer readings (specific gravity values) of the solution in each of the cells. The method of doing this is shown in Fig. 24. The Lucas hydrometer contains a graduated float which indicates the specific gravity of the battery cell from which a sample of the electrolyte is taken.

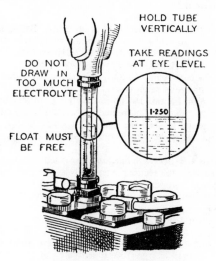

DO NOT DRAW IN TOO MUCH ELECTROLYTE

HOLD TUBE VERTICALLY

TAKE READINGS AT EYE LEVEL

1·250

FLOAT MUST BE FREE

Fig. 24. Checking specific gravity of electrolyte in Lucas battery

After a sample has been taken and checked, it must, of course, be returned to the cell. The taking of specific gravity readings with a hydrometer is the most efficient way of ascertaining the state of charge of the battery. The specific gravity readings should be approximately the *same for all three cells*. Should the reading for one cell differ substantially from the readings for the others, probably some acid has been spilled or has leaked from the cell concerned. There is also a possibility of a short-circuit between the battery plates. In the latter case is will be necessary to return the battery to a Lucas service depot for attention.

Under no circumstances must the battery be permitted to remain in a discharged condition for long, or serious deterioration will occur. After checking the specific gravity readings and topping-up the cells, wipe the top of the battery and remove any spilled electrolyte or water; replace all the filler plugs and the battery lid. Then fit and tighten the battery clamping bolt.

Lucas Battery Connections. Keep the battery connections clean, free from corrosion, and tight, otherwise the ammeter readings will *not* indicate the true state of charge of the battery. To prevent corrosion both connections should be smeared with petroleum jelly. Note that a "positive earth" system is used and if the battery is removed, the terminals must be correctly reconnected. The coloured lead must be connected to the battery negative (—) terminal.

Specific Gravity. With Lucas batteries on B.S.A. Bantams, the specific gravity readings at an acid temperature of approximately 60°F should be: 1·280–1·300, battery fully charged; about 1·210 battery, about half discharged; about 1·110–1·150, battery fully discharged.

Never leave the battery in a discharged state for any appreciable period. A low state of charge is often caused through parking the machine for long periods with the lighting switch in the "L" position, unaccompanied by much daylight running. The remedy is, of course, to undertake more daylight running and to keep the switch in the OFF position as much as possible until the battery regains its normal state of charge.

Running Minus a Battery. On machines provided with a battery it is important to disconnect the rectifier completely at the snap connectors and to insulate all leads properly from each other and from earth, prior to running with the battery removed. Do not switch on the lights with the engine running, otherwise all bulbs will fuse and there is a risk of the rectifier being burnt out.

Storage. If Lucas equipment is laid by for some months, the battery must be given a small charge from a separate source of electrical energy about once a month, in order to obviate any permanent sulphation of the plates. In no circumstances must the electrolyte be removed from the battery and the plates allowed to dry, as certain chemical changes take place which result in permanent loss of capacity.

The Varley MC 5/9 Battery. This five-plate, 6-volt, 9 amp-hr battery is used on 1954–5 Bantams with Wipac battery-lighting (and on a.c. sets converted to d.c.). It is a "dry" lead-acid type and has some definite advantages over the "free acid" type. The whole of the necessary electrolyte is completely absorbed and held in suspension by the porous plates and separator material which together form a block completely filling all space in the battery container. The battery has no free acid to spill, is unaffected by vibration, corrodes very gradually, has a big useful life, and requires a negligible amount of maintenance.

Maintenance of the Varley Battery. Provided that the Bantam is taken out regularly for daylight runs, the generator will maintain the battery in a good state of charge. But *once a month* it is desirable to top-up the battery.

Always keep the battery connections clean and tight and the positive terminal earthed. See that the upper part of the battery (below the lid) is kept quite clean and dry. Make sure that all the filler plugs have their rubber washers intact and properly positioned. Also verify that the vent holes are unobstructed. Check the above points when topping-up the battery. If the battery is permitted to stand idle for a considerable period, you should give it a freshening charge about once a month.

To Top-up the Varley Battery. To maintain the plates and separators in a moist condition, top-up (monthly) the cells, using about a *teaspoonful* of distilled water per cell. Top-up *after*, and not before a run. After allowing the battery to stand for a quarter of an hour, remove all surplus liquid with a small syringe or by shaking out. This is most important.

Voltage and State of Charge. The following voltages shown by a moving coil voltmeter indicate the approximate state of charge of the Varley MC 5/9 battery:

Fully discharged: 5·7 volts or under
Partially discharged: 6·15 volts or under
Open circuit fully charged: 6·3 volts or over
On charge, fully charged: 7·8 volts or over

Bench Charging Varley Battery. Should bench charging be necessary, note that the normal charge rate is 1 amp. When the voltage reading on charge reaches 7·8 volts, continue to charge for a further three hours. Charging for twelve hours at 1 amp is normally sufficient.

If the battery becomes abnormally dry, top-up with distilled water before and during charging. Subsequently remove all surplus liquid.

If the capacity of the battery falls after the battery has been in use for a considerable time, it may be necessary to top-up with weak sulphuric *acid* (1·100 S.G.) instead of distilled water, for one or two bench charges.

THE RECTIFIER

In the case of Lucas (1950–3) and Wipac (1954–70) battery-lighting equipment, the rectifier itself is responsible for converting the alternating current produced by the generator into direct (unidirectional) current for battery charging. It is important to see that the rectifier always makes good contact with its support, the rectifier being cooled by surface contact.

Maintenance. Provided that the rectifier leads are securely attached to the rectifier, no maintenance of any kind is required, and the rectifier (attached to the toolbox bracket below the saddle or between the toolbox and battery) should not be interfered with. If any trouble occurs, return the complete unit to the nearest B.S.A. or Wipac agent. Avoid obstructing the air flow to the rectifier by fitting any additional accessories, or stowing personal belongings, beneath the saddle or dualseat.

Note particularly that the electrical equipment (and especially the rectifier) on the B.S.A. Bantam is specifically designed for use with the "positive earth" system, and the *positive* terminal of the battery must always be *earthed*. Therefore when it is necessary to remove the battery from the machine, it must always be replaced with the positive terminal properly earthed. Incorrect connecting up of the battery leads will immediately result in the complete burning out of the rectifier. The exception to this is certain D1 and D3 models where a "negative earth" system was employed (*see* page 77).

THE LAMPS

Lucas lamps are specified on 1950–3 Model D1 Bantams with battery lighting and coil ignition. On 1948–65 models with direct lighting and ignition, Wipac lamps are used exclusively; several different types of headlamp have been specified. The headlamp fitted to 1954–70 Bantams having battery lighting is also of Wipac design. Note that a Wipac stop–tail light is available only for Wipac battery-lighting models.

The Lucas SSP575P Headlamp (1950–3). This Lucas headlamp has a double-filament main bulb and a pilot bulb. The main bulb is a "pre-focus" type which requires *no focusing adjustment*, the filament being permanently positioned in focus relatively to the reflector. One filament of the double-filament main bulb is responsible for the main driving beam, while the other filament (controlled by a dipper switch on the handlebars) provides a dipped beam for riding in foggy weather and when passing oncoming vehicles.

The Lucas headlamp embodies a Lucas "light unit" comprising a combined reflector, bulb holder, and front lens assembly. On 1950–1 models (and up to March, 1952) the pilot bulb is mounted at the rear of the light unit (*see* Fig. 25) and shines through a transparent window in the reflector. The 1952–3 Lucas headlamp has an underslung pilot light, the bulb being mounted vertically downwards on a carrier plate at the base of the lamp shell (*F*, Fig. 26) and shining through an external window beneath the reflector.

Lighting Switch Positions on Lucas Headlamp. See the appropriate information given on page 9.

Warming Up of Lucas Headlamp Shell. Should the headlamp shell become warm while riding by day with the lamps off, do not suspect a fault in the wiring. The condition is quite normal and is caused through the reduced-charge resistance G (in headlamp shell) dispersing some of the energy from the generator in the form of heat, thus causing a rise in the temperature of the headlamp shell.

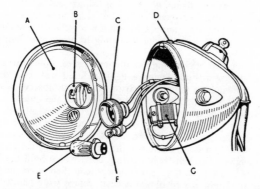

Fig. 25. Lucas "Pre-focus" type headlamp with pilot bulb fitted internally (1950–1)

The Lucas light-unit assembly is shown removed from the headlamp

Key to Figs. 25, 26

A. *Reflector of light unit*
B. *Bulb holder*
C. *Adapter*
D. *Lamp front securing-screw*

E. *Main bulb*
F. *Pilot bulb (carrier plate, Fig. 26)*
G. *Reduced charge resistance*

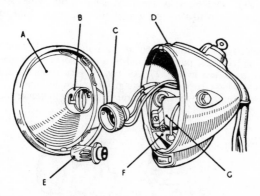

Fig. 26. Lucas "Pre-focus" headlamp with underslung pilot light (1952–3)

In this instance also, the light-unit assembly is shown removed

Aligning Lucas Headlamp. No focusing adjustment is called for as the headlamp is of the "pre-focus" type, but it is sometimes desirable to check the alignment of the lamp. Unless this is correct, the best illumination is unobtainable and some dazzle, annoying to other road users, may be caused.

The best method of checking the alignment is to stand your Bantam in its normal riding attitude facing a light-coloured wall at a distance of about 25 ft. Switch on the main driving light and observe whether the beam is projected straight ahead and parallel with the ground.

With a tape measure or a piece of string, take vertical measurements from the centre of the headlamp, and from the centre of the illuminated circular patch on the wall, to the ground. Both measurements should be the same. If they are unequal, obviously the headlamp is tilted and must be correctly aligned. Slacken both securing bolts which hold the headlamp between the brackets on the front-fork legs, and then move the headlamp up or down as required to obtain a beam centre truly parallel with the ground. Finally, retighten the two lamp securing bolts firmly.

To Remove Lucas Lamp Front. With a screwdriver slacken the small plated screw on top of the headlamp shell (*D*, Figs. 25 and 26), withdraw the rim, complete with light-unit assembly, outward from the top; as the light-unit *A* emerges, raise it slightly to free the lower metal tongue from the headlamp shell.

To replace the lamp front (light-unit assembly), locate the small metal tongue on the headlamp rim with the corresponding slot at the bottom of the lamp shell, and carefully press the lamp front home. Afterwards secure in position by tightening the small securing screw at the top of the rim.

The Lucas 480 Tail Lamp (1950–3). To remove the shell of the lamp carrying the red glass, push it in and turn *anti-clockwise*. It can then be withdrawn as shown in Fig. 27. As may be seen from the sketch, the bulb itself also has a bayonet type fixing. To replace the lamp shell, engage the bayonet fixing, push in, and then turn clockwise to secure the shell to the flanged body of the lamp.

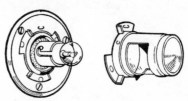

Fig. 27. The Lucas 480 tail lamp

Fitted to 1950–3 Bantams with Lucas battery-lighting

The Lucas Stop–Tail Lamp. Some 1952 and all 1953 Bantams with Lucas battery-lighting equipment have a Lucas stop–tail lamp provided instead of the ordinary tail lamp. To remove the red "Diacon"-plastic portion of the lamp and obtain access to the double-filament bulb, it is only necessary to remove the two securing screws.

Lucas Replacement Bulbs. It is preferable to renew bulbs after considerable service and before the filaments actually burn out, as this prevents deterioration of illumination caused through sagging of the filaments. Always use Lucas bulbs in Lucas lamps for which they are specially designed and tested. All Lucas bulbs have their metal caps marked with a number for identification, and when renewing a bulb see that the number on the cap (e.g. 200, 312, 988) is correct for the particular bulb concerned.

In a 1950–3 "pre-focus" Lucas headlamp use a 6-volt 30/24 watt, Lucas No. 312 double-filament main bulb. This has a broad locating flange on the cap and cannot be fitted wrongly, i.e. with the dipped-beam filament *below* the driving-light filament. A groove in the bulb flange engages a projection in the bulb holder.

In the case of the headlamp pilot light, fit a Lucas 6-volt, 3-watt, No. 988 bulb. In the tail lamp use a 6-volt, 6-watt, Lucas No. 205 bulb. The pilot and tail lamp bulbs have a bayonet type fixing. If a Lucas stop–tail lamp (similar in design to the tail lamp shown in Fig. 27) is specified, fit a 6-volt, 6/18-watt, Lucas No. 352 double-filament bulb which has offset securing pins to prevent incorrect fitting.

Fitting Bulbs to Lucas Headlamp. With the Lucas "pre-focus" type headlamp, to obtain access to the main and pilot bulbs for bulb renewal, remove the Lucas lamp front as described (page 68). Next, to remove the double-filament main bulb, turn the adaptor (*C*, Figs. 25, 26) *anti-clockwise* and pull it off. Then lift the "pre-focus" bulb *E* out of the bulb holder *B*. It is quite free once the adaptor has been removed.

On the 1950–1 headlamp, to remove the pilot bulb release the bayonet fixing securing the bulb (*F*, Fig. 25) to the holder on the adaptor. On the 1952–3 headlamp with underslung pilot light, slide the horizontal carrier plate (*F*, Fig. 26) inside the lamp out of its locating groove, and release the bayonet fixing of the bulb.

To renew a double-filament main bulb, fit the correct renewal bulb (*see* above) into the bulb holder (dipped-beam filament uppermost), engage the two projections on the inside of the adaptor with the slots in the bulb holder, press on, and secure by turning *clockwise*.

The Wipac 1–58 Headlamp (1948–51). This sturdy and thoroughly weatherproof headlamp has been fitted to Bantams with Wipac direct ignition and lighting up to January 1952. It has a double-filament main bulb supplied direct with current from the Wipac generator and pilot bulb above the main bulb for parking purposes; the pilot bulb is supplied with current from a bicycle-type dry battery inside the headlamp behind the reflector.

There is no focusing adjustment for the main bulb, the bulb being permanently in correct focus. But it is, of course, possible to align the headlamp in the front fork brackets. No external lighting switch is fitted to the headlamp, all switch components being totally enclosed inside the body of the lamp. The switch is therefore most unlikely to be affected by the weather. The switch (including the dipper circuit) is remote-controlled by a Bowden cable having its operating lever (*see* Fig. 28), conveniently mounted on the near side of the handlebars.

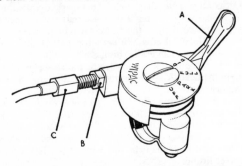

Fig. 28. Handlebar lighting switch for Wipac 1–58 headlamp
(1948–51)

A. *Switch lever*   B. *Lock-nut*   C. *Adjuster for synchronizing*

Lighting Switch Positions for Wipac 1–58 Headlamp. The four consecutive lever positions of the remote-control switch lever fitted to 1948–51 Bantams are explained on page 9.

Adjustment of Remote-control Switch Lever. An adjustment of the remote-control switch lever for the Wipac 1–58 headlamp is seldom called for. But should the switch lever (shown at *A* in Fig. 28) ever need an adjustment to synchronize the lever movement with the action of the switch itself inside the headlamp, this can readily be effected as described below.

First check that the two lamp bulbs fitted are serviceable. Next place the Bantam on its central stand, start up the engine, and allow it to tick-over at a moderate speed. Move the lever *A* (Fig. 28) to the "FULL" position, and then slacken the lock-nut *B*, and while observing the headlamp, with a suitable spanner screw the adjuster *C* in or out as required to obtain the driving beam. Afterwards tighten the lock-nut *B* securely. If perfect synchronizing is obtained with the switch in the "FULL" position, the cable should be correctly aligned for the three remaining positions marked on the handlebar lever. It is, however, advisable to move the lever through *all* its positions and verify whether the headlamp switch responds.

Should no lighting occur with the lever in a certain position, leave the lever in this position, slacken the lock-nut *B* (Fig. 28) again, and with great care make a further adjustment with the adjuster *C* until the light appears. Retighten the lock-nut and move the lever back into the "FULL" position to confirm that the operating cable has not been moved too far from its initial setting. Should it have done so, once more repeat the adjustment, but turn the adjuster as required with the greatest caution.

Aligning Wipac 1–58 Headlamp. *See* page 68, "Aligning Lucas Headlamp."

To Remove Wipac 1–58 Lamp Front. The front rim of the headlamp houses the reflector and bulb-assembly bracket, and the parking battery is inside the lamp body at the rear. To obtain access to the bulbs and dry battery slacken the slotted screw at the base of the headlamp rim, and withdraw the lamp front outwards and upwards. On the 1948 headlamp the front has a hinge and spring clip, and the front can be gently pulled off.

The Wipac 1–59 Tail Lamp (1948–50). To remove the rim of the 1–59 tail lamp carrying the red glass, unscrew the small 6BA locking screw under the lamp and then turn the rim anti-clockwise and withdraw. The bulb holder has a bayonet type fixing for the bulb which can be instantly removed by the usual "push and-turn" method.

Note that the replacement for the 1–59 tail lamp fitted to 1948–50 Bantams has a $1\frac{1}{2}$ in. diameter rear window and 6-watt bulb, to comply with 1955 rear light regulations. The Part No. of the modified tail lamp is 05160.

To Renew Parking Battery (Wipac 1–58 Headlamp). Remove the parking battery from inside the headlamp as soon as it is discharged. If it is permitted to remain in the lamp, it will corrode and spoil the body of the headlamp. Obtain a 3-volt twin-cell bicycle-lamp dry battery, type 800, and hold it so that the vertical contact strip faces towards the headlamp. Then locate the battery upside down in the support bracket so that the vertical contact connects with the metal battery holder at the rear of the headlamp. See that the horizontal contact-strip rests on top of the lower contact.

Wipac Replacement Bulbs. Renew bulbs before they burn right out (*see* page 69). With a.c. direct lighting equipment it is essential to fit bulbs of the correct wattage. For 1948–61 Wipac 1–58 and 1–58F headlamps, fit a 6-volt, 24/24-watt, double-filament main bulb, and a 2·5-volt, 0·25-amp parking bulb. Where a tail lamp is concerned, use a 6-volt, 6-watt, single-filament, double-contact bulb. For a pre-1954 stop–tail lamp, use a 6-volt,

6/18-watt bulb (*see also* page 75). The correct speedometer bulb is a 6·5-volt 0·3-amp, 1·95-watt type. The caps on all except pilot and speedometer bulbs (screw type) have a bayonet fixing.

Fitting Bulbs to Wipac 1–58 Headlamp (1948–51). To gain access to the headlamp bulbs, remove the lamp front as previously described. To remove the bulb-assembly bracket, bend downwards the small tabs which project from the base of the reflector. Then remove the bulb assembly bracket by turning it slightly anti-clockwise. The double-filament main bulb and the parking bulb are now readily accessible, and can be removed for inspection and renewal if necessary.

When fitting a new double-filament main bulb it is essential to check that the word "TOP" marked on the bulb is in fact at the top. Should the bulb be unmarked, you must fit it in accordance with the diagram shown in Fig. 29, i.e. with the offset (dip) filament uppermost.

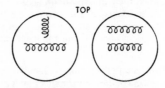

Fig. 29. Wipac main bulbs must always be fitted like this
(1948–61 models)

The offset filament for dipping must be uppermost as indicated

The Wipac 1–58F Headlamp (1952–61). This type of a.c. headlamp (*see* Fig. 30) is specified on the 1952–61 Bantams provided with Wipac direct-lighting equipment. The rotary-type switch on top of the headlamp (introduced in January, 1952) is the main difference between this headlamp and the earlier (type 1–58) headlamp fitted to 1948–51 direct-lighting models with remote-control lighting switch on the handlebars. On this headlamp the pilot bulb is below the main bulb.

The 1–58 headlamp has a double-filament main bulb supplied with current direct from the lighting coils of the S55/Mk. 8 a.c./d.c. generator. A pilot bulb is fitted below the main bulb for parking purposes, and this is fed with current from a bicycle-type dry battery inside the headlamp behind the reflector.

There is no adjustment for main-bulb focus, but the headlamp can be tilted fore and aft for alignment, in the front-fork support brackets. The rotary-type lighting switch on top of the headlamp shell has three positions, namely OFF, L, H. When the switch is in the H position, the main driving beam can be dipped when required by means of a dipper switch on the handlebars.

To remove the lamp front see details for 1–58 lamp on page 71.

The Wipac 02143 Headlamp (1954–61). This d.c. headlamp on most 1954–61 Model D1, D3 Bantams with battery lighting is basically of similar design to the Wipac 1–58F headlamp already dealt with and illustrated in Fig. 30. The rotary lighting switch has the same three positions, and an ignition key is omitted because current for ignition is taken direct from the

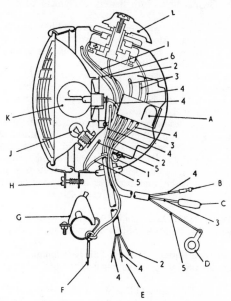

Fig. 30. Sectional drawing of a Wipac 1–58F headlamp (1952–61)

This headlamp is fitted to direct-lighting models. The rotary-type switch replaces the remote-control switch shown in Fig. 28, used in conjunction with the 1948–51 Wipac 1–58 headlamp.

A. Parking battery (dry)
B. Generator lead
C. Tail lamp lead
D. Earth lead
E. Dipper-switch group
F. Speedometer lead

G. Dipper switch (handlebar fitting)
H. Lamp-front fixing screw
J. Parking bulb
K. Double-filament main bulb
L. Lighting switch

1. Green
2. Light red
3. Black

4. Dark red
5. Translucent
6. Blue

S55/Mk. 8 generator (No. IG 1130 d.c.). The essential difference is in regard to the switch wiring, two leads being taken to the rectifier. Also the internal parking battery is omitted, the pilot bulb being fed direct from the battery.

1960–70 Wipac Headlamps. These are similar to earlier type Wipac headlamps but have pre-focus double-filament main bulbs. The main bulbs are 6-volt, 24/24 watt (30/24 watt from 1967 onwards.) No focusing adjustment is possible or necessary and a prefocus bulb cannot be fitted incorrectly. On machines with a direct lighting set fit a 2·5-volt, 0·25-amp parking bulb. On machines with battery equipment fit a 6-volt, 3-watt parking bulb.

The lamp front, together with the reflector and bulb assembly, is secured to the lamp casing by a slotted screw above or below the headlamp according to model. To remove a bulb it is therefore only necessary to loosen the slotted screw until you can withdraw the rim.

To replace the double-filament pre-focus main bulb, press the bulb retainer inwards and turn it slightly anti-clockwise. Then lift the retainer off and withdraw the bulb. Note that a new bulb automatically provides correct relationship of the two filaments.

To check that the headlamp beam is projected straight ahead and is parallel with the ground, position the Bantam, off its stand, about 25 feet away from a light-coloured wall. The height of the beam centre on the wall should be the same as the height of the headlamp centre. If it is not, move the lamp as required after slackening the bolts securing the headlamp. On models where the lamp front is secured to a nacelle (which replaces the lamp body) it is necessary to slacken two screws on the nacelle rim.

To Align Wipac 1–58F Headlamp (1948–61). Observe the instructions given on page 68 for the Lucas SSP575P headlamp.

To Renew Parking Battery (Wipac 1–58F Headlamp). Do this in accordance with the instructions given on page 71 for the 1–58 headlamp.

The Wipac 1–93 Tail Lamp (1951–3). To remove the half of the lamp carrying the red plastic, push in, turn anti-clockwise, and remove. This gives access to the bulb (single filament, a.c.; double filament, d.c.), which has the usual bayonet-type fixing and can instantly be withdrawn. When refitting the lamp half, engage the bayonet fixing, push in and turn clockwise.

The Wipac 1A–93 Stop–Tail Lamp (1950–3). Some 1950–3 D1's provided with Wipac battery lighting equipment[1] have a 1A–93 stop–tail lamp fitted instead of the 1–93 tail lamp. The Wipac 1A–93 stop–tail lamp is identical to the 1–93 tail lamp except that two wires and connectors are attached to the lamp, which has a single 6-volt, 6/18-watt double-filament bulb.

One filament, connected direct through the lighting switch, illuminates the red tail light, and the other one is illuminated only by the stop-light switch

---

[1] Wipac stop–tail lamps and switches are not designed or available for use on Bantams having a.c. flywheel generators giving direct lighting.

when the rear brake is applied. To remove the unit carrying the red glass, and to withdraw the double filament bulb, follow the instructions already given for the Wipac 1–93 tail lamp.

The Wipac 110 Stop–Tail Lamp (1954–62). Late 1954 Bantams (Models D1 and D3) with Wipac battery lighting, and all 1955–62 Bantams, are fitted with the Wipac 110 stop–tail lamp. On 1955–62 machines with direct lighting, the two stop-light bulbs are, of course, omitted. The 110 lamp can also be used as a replacement for the 1–93 and 1A–93 lamps.

The Wipac 110 stop–tail lamp comprises two parts, a back-plate and a red polystyrene plastic cover. As may be seen in Fig. 31, the back-plate has three bulbs. For the stop warning-lights (operated by the rear-brake pedal) two 6-volt, 3-watt screw-type bulbs are fitted on either side of a 6-volt, 6-watt bayonet fitting tail light bulb. With this bulb combination, renewal of the bulbs is much cheaper than is the case where a double-filament bulb is provided. The red polystyrene plastic cover has three "bull's eyes" located in line with the three bulbs, thereby giving penetrating illumination.

To remove the plastic cover from the 110 lamp, remove the two countersunk screws securing the cover to the back-plate. This exposes the three bulbs as shown in Fig. 31. To remove the 3-watt tail-lamp bulb, push the

Fig. 31. The back-plate of the Wipac 110 stop–tail lamp (1954–62)

An unusual method of mounting the bulbs is used. On 1955–62 Bantams with direct lighting, the two stop-light bulbs are omitted

bulb sideways in its spring clip. To remove the 6-watt stop-light bulbs, unscrew the bulbs from the holders which are in the form of coil springs. These act as self locking devices when the bulbs are screwed home.

Wipac Stop–Tail Lamps (1963–6). On 1963–5 Bantams a Wipac 143 stop–tail lamp is fitted, very similar to the Wipac 110 lamp shown in Fig. 31.

On all except direct lighting models two 6-volt, 6-watt stop-light bulbs are fitted, one on each side of the 6-volt, 3-watt tail lamp bulb. On 1963–5 models with direct lighting the two stop-light bulbs are, of course, omitted. All 1966–70 Bantams have a Wipac 143B stop–tail lamp with a single 6-volt, 3/18-watt double-filament bulb. Access to the bulb or bulbs on all 1963–70 stop–tail lamps is obtained by unscrewing two countersunk screws and removing the transparent red plastic portion of the lamp.

Renewing Bulbs (Wipac 1–58F Headlamp, 1–93 Tail Lamp). The headlamp bulbs can be withdrawn without disturbing the reflector, and the whole of the instructions given on pages 72 and 74 apply. Be careful to fit the headlamp double-filament main bulb the correct way round (*see* Fig. 29). Bulb renewals as on page 72.

Alignment, Bulb Renewal, etc. (Wipac 02143 Headlamp.) Use the previous instructions given for the 1–58F headlamp disregarding all reference to the parking battery, and noting that a 6-volt, 3-watt pilot bulb is required instead of the 2·5-volt, 0·25-amp parking bulb referred to on page 74.

Care of Wipac Headlamps (1948–70). Very little attention is required. Occasionally verify that the wiring connectors are gripping the leads firmly, and check that the securing bolts on both sides of the headlamp body are firmly tightened. Always keep the glass front perfectly clean. If it is permitted to become dirty, the brilliance of the headlamp beam will necessarily be affected.

Improved Dipper Switch for 1951–2 Bantams. As has been mentioned on page 9, the series 1–102 dipper switch fitted to 1951–2 Bantams provided with direct lighting and ignition (and the S55/Mk. 8 generator) is rather sensitive to varying finger pressures which can cause momentary overloading of the lighting circuit. The trouble can be simply rectified by scrapping the series 1–102 dipper switch and fitting in its place the modified series 96 switch. This improved switch can be obtained from the Wipac Group Sales Ltd.

WIRING OF EQUIPMENT

It is rarely necessary to interfere with the wiring harness, and normally no attention is needed throughout the useful life of the motor-cycle, provided that the owner is not very careless or neglectful of the electrical components and does not leave the machine in the open unprotected.

Some useful wiring diagrams are included (Figs. 32–39) in this section for the benefit of those who may have to attend to the wiring at some time or other.

Keep All Connections Tight. Occasionally verify that all connections to the electrical components are tight and that all rubber shields, where provided, are pulled properly over the connections. The various connections can be readily identified by referring to the appropriate wiring diagram.

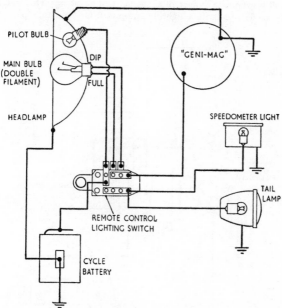

Fig. 32. Wiring diagram for 1948–50 Model D1 Bantams with Wipac a.c. "Geni-mag" and Wipac 1–58 headlamp with handlebar lighting switch

This diagram applies to 123 cm³ Bantams with Wipac direct lighting from 1948 up to August, 1950

Battery Leads on d.c. Equipment. It is important to note that on nearly all 1950–66 Bantams fitted with battery lighting, the *positive* terminal of the battery is earthed. If it is necessary for any reason to disconnect the battery leads, it is essential afterwards to reconnect them correctly, i.e. with the positive (+) to earth. As has been mentioned on page 10, the rectifier will suffer serious damage if the battery leads are accidentally reversed.

Where Wipac battery-lighting equipment is fitted to Models D1 and D3 Bantams prior to engine numbers DDB–101 and BD3B–5001 respectively, a multi-plate rectifier is used with a *negative* earth. On all later Wipac battery models the rectifier is of the enclosed single-unit "pancake" type, with the *positive* terminal earthed.

Attention to Lucas Wiring. Before making any alterations to the wiring on machines with Lucas equipment (or removing the panel housing the lighting switch), always disconnect the negative lead from the battery. This will prevent the danger of a short circuit occurring. This also applies to 1954–66 Wipac battery lighting equipment (*see* previous paragraphs).

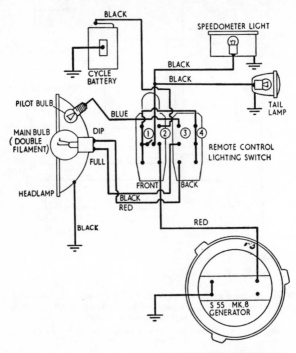

Fig. 33. Wiring diagram for 1950–1 Model D1 Bantams with Wipac a.c./d.c. S55/Mk. 8 generator and Wipac 1–58 headlamp with handlebar lighting switch

This diagram applies to 123 cm³ Bantams with Wipac direct lighting from August, 1950, to December, 1951, inclusive

The negative lead from the battery (approximately one foot in length) is connected to the lead from the lighting switch by a brass connector. A rubber shield insulates the connector which must never be permitted to touch the frame or other metal part of the machine. Should there be such contact, the battery will immediately be short-circuited. To unscrew the

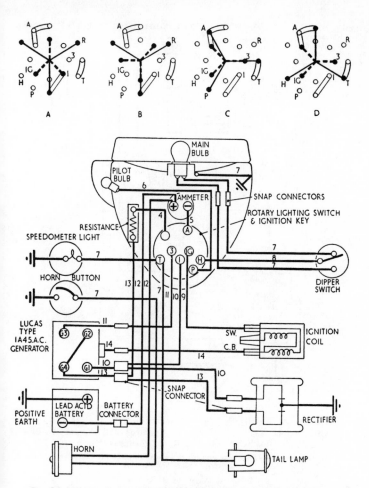

Fig. 34. Wiring diagram for 1950–3 Model D1 Bantams with Lucas
a.c. generator and Lucas SSP575P headlamp with headlamp
lighting switch

*This diagram applies to 123 cm³ Bantams with Lucas battery-lighting (rectifier) and coil
ignition, provided as an alternative to the Wipac direct-lighting equipment*

4. Brown and yellow
5. Brown and blue
6. Red and black
7. Black
8. Blue
9. White

10. Purple
11. Green
12. Brown
13. Yellow
14. White and black

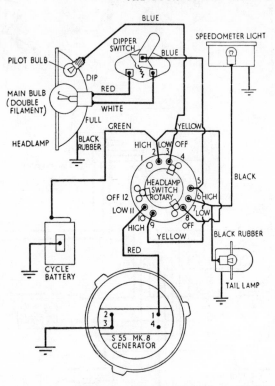

Fig. 35. Wiring diagram for 1952–61 Models D1 and D3 Bantams with Wipac a.c./d.c. S55/Mk. 8 generator and Wipac 1–58F headlamp with headlamp lighting switch

This diagram applies to 123 cm³ and 148 cm³ Bantams with Wipac direct lighting from January, 1952, to 1959 inclusive

brass connector it is, of course, necessary first to push back the rubber shield. After reconnecting the lead, make quite sure that the rubber shield is pulled well over the brass connector.

WIPAC ELECTRIC HORN

On Bantams having Wipac battery-lighting and direct-ignition equipment the electric horn is very carefully adjusted by the makers to give maximum performance, and it is rarely necessary to attend to the horn in any way until a very big mileage has been covered.

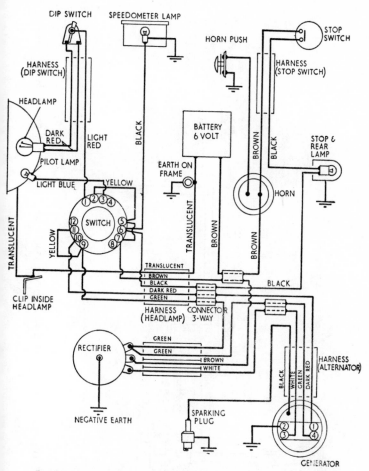

Fig. 36. Wiring diagram for 1954–61 Models D1, D3, D5 Bantams with Wipac 02143 headlamp and Wipac a.c./d.c. S55/Mk. 8 generator

On late 1954 and all 1955–61 battery lighting models the battery positive terminal is earthed and a three-bulb stop–tail lamp is fitted. On 1960–1 models the Wipac type 0213 headlamp was replaced by a Wipac type SO891 headlamp with a "pre-focus" main bulb. The above diagram, however, applies to all models

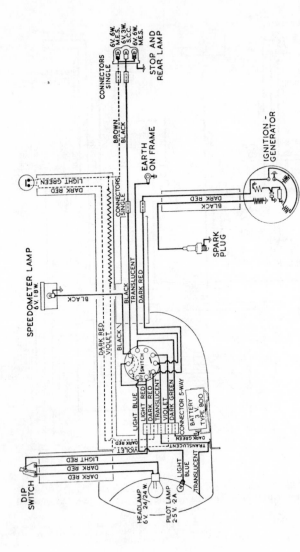

Fig. 37. Wiring diagram for 1962–5 direct lighting Models D7, D7D/L with Wipac a.c./d.c. S55/Mk. 8 generator and Wipac SO856 headlamp

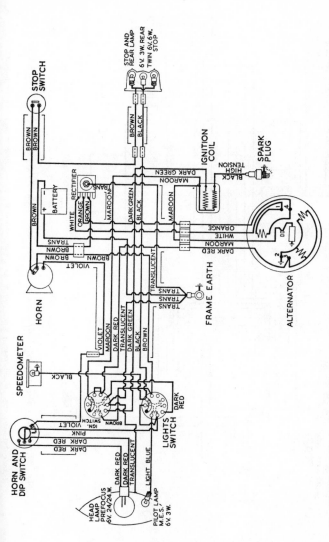

Fig. 38. Wiring diagram for 1962–6 coil ignition and battery lighting models D7, D7D/L with Wipac S55/Mk. 8 generator and Wipac SO891 headlamp

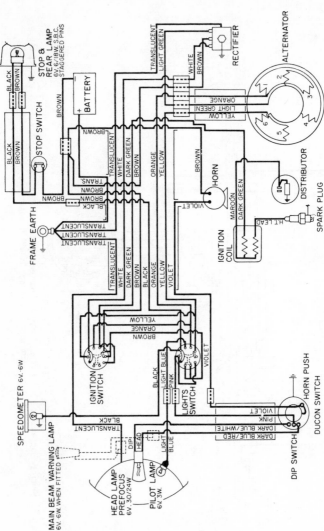

Fig. 39. Wiring diagram for 1967–70 coil-ignition and battery-lighting models D10, D14, and Bantam 175

Note that some cable colours (notably those from the generator) have changed from those on the preceding diagrams

If the Horn Becomes Ineffective. In the event of the horn becoming uncertain in action, failing to vibrate, or emitting only a choking sound, do not conclude immediately that the horn itself has failed. Verify that the horn trouble is not caused by some external source such as a loose connection, a short circuit in the wiring, or a discharged condition of the battery. Also check that the horn securing-bolt has not slackened off. This can interfere with the action of the horn.

To Adjust the Horn. Should it be found impossible to rectify poor horn action by checking the points mentioned in the previous paragraph, you can effect an adjustment of the horn in the following manner. First remove the rubber plug from the body of the horn. This exposes the adjuster screw. Then to make the required adjustment, turn the adjuster screw slightly clockwise or anti-clockwise while actuating the horn button, until an effective horn note is obtained. Afterwards replace the rubber plug in the horn body. If horn trouble persists in spite of all efforts to rectify it, return the complete horn to Wipac Group Sales Ltd., London Road, Buckingham, Bucks., or to one of their service stations for expert attention.

6 General maintenance

All essential instructions are given in this chapter concerning the normal maintenance, dismantling, and assembling required for 1948 and subsequent Bantams. Detailed reference is not made, however, to lubrication, carburation, the ignition system, and the lighting equipment, because these matters have already been fully covered in earlier chapters. This chapter has been subdivided into a number of main sections to enable the reader to refer quickly to any specific information.

Repairs and Spares. When it is necessary to forward or deliver parts to the makers (B.S.A. Motor Cycles Ltd., Service Dept., Armoury Road, Birmingham, 11), or to an appointed B.S.A. dealer, always remember to attach to each part a label bearing clearly your full name and address. Any correspondence about technical advice and repairs should always be written on *separate* sheets to ensure its being attended to with the minimum delay. To help identification, always quote the year of Bantam manufacture and model number. Also quote the corresponding engine or frame number (*see* footnote on page 1), accordingly.

A handy illustrated spares list is obtainable from any appointed B.S.A. spares stockist who keeps a comprehensive range of B.S.A. spares.

Items Needed for Maintenance. You *must* have handy in the garage or lock-up certain items besides those in the Bantam tool kit. They include: a can of paraffin for cleaning purposes; a stiff brush for scouring dirt off the crankcase and underneath the motor-cycle; a tin of suitable engine oil for the engine and gearbox (*see* page 20); a funnel for topping-up the gearbox; a canister of grease (*see* page 20); a receptacle for oil when draining the crankcase; a drip-tray; some dishes or jars in which to wash parts when dismantling; some non-fluffy rags; some fine emery cloth; a pair of new gudgeon-pin circlips.

A proprietary gudgeon-pin extractor may also prove useful, and it is desirable to obtain a small pair of snipe-nosed pliers for removing gudgeon-pin circlips; a small wire brush for cleaning plug threads, etc.; a Champion combined feeler gauge and plug regapping tool (*see* page 47); a suitable feeler gauge for checking the contact-breaker gap.

For the maintenance of the motor-cycle parts, you should obtain: a tyre-pressure gauge (*see* page 103); a tyre repair outfit; an extra tyre lever;

a box of spare chain links and a chain-rivet extractor; a Lucas battery filler (*see* page 62) or a small syringe for topping-up the battery on a Bantam fitted with a Lucas or Varley battery respectively; a chamois leather; a sponge and pail (if a hose is not available); some soft dusters (preferably of the Selvyt type): a tin of good wax or other proprietary polish for the enamelled parts; and last but not least, a tin of good hand cleanser.

Tools for Repair Work. In the event of your deciding to tackle as much repair work as possible besides normal routine maintenance, stripping-down, and assembly, it is advisable to rig up a suitable bench, complete with vice, and also to buy a steel rule and a few additional tools.

To commence with it is a good plan to purchase a good screwdriver; a medium-weight hammer, a small hand-drill, some twist drills, a hacksaw, some large and small (smooth and rough) files, and a reliable soldering outfit for repairing broken control cables. Major repair work necessitates considerable skill in the handling of tools, and some sound engineering knowledge. Without these you are not advised to attempt any major repair work on the power unit or machine.

If reconditioning of the engine and gearbox unit is undertaken, you will require some special service tools, among which may well be mentioned: No. 61–3188 for removing the generator flywheel (models prior to 1967); extractor No. 61–3796 for removing the engine sprocket; No. 61–3191 for removing the clutch plate circlip; No. 61–3256 for extracting the clutch hub; various other punches, reamers, etc.

Details of Bantam service tools, and helpful repair unstructions (such as how to part the flywheels and drive out the crankpin) are included in the B.S.A. service sheets Nos. 505, 506, 508, 509, etc., obtainable from B.S.A. spares stockists. Bantam repair work, is, of course, quite outside the scope of this maintenance handbook. One B.S.A. service tool likely to interest the average Bantam owner is No. 61–3191 (shown in use in Fig. 57) for compressing the clutch springs to enable the clutch-plate assembly to be withdrawn for inspection and the friction inserts and springs renewed if necessary.

Keep Your Bantam Clean. If bought new, it cost quite an appreciable sum, and it is well worth looking after carefully. If cleaned regularly and properly, it will run better, last longer, keep its good looks, and retain a good second-hand value in the event of your ever wishing to sell it. A dirty Bantam is an eyesore. Furthermore, dirt covers defects, accelerates rusting, and is a nuisance and a menace when dismantling. On no account leave your Bantam soaking wet overnight. If you cannot spare the time for cleaning the machine in wet weather, grease it all over before using it.

Cleaning the Power Unit. Always keep the cylinder barrel and light-alloy cylinder-head fins clean. If the barrel fins are rusted, clean them with a stiff brush dipped in paraffin and afterwards paint the fins with some proprietary cylinder black. Rusted cylinder-barrel fins, besides giving a shabby look to the engine, cause an appreciable loss in heat dispersion.

Scour off all filth from the lower part of the engine and gearbox unit with stiff brushes and paraffin. Thoroughly clean all aluminium alloy and bright surfaces with a rag damped in paraffin, helped by brushes where necessary.

To Clean the Enamel. Do not attempt to remove mud from the enamelled parts when dry and caked, as this is liable to scratch the surfaces. If available, use a hose carefully to soak the mud off. If a machine is very dirty, it may be advisable to paint the surfaces over with a cleaning compound such as "Gunk" before directing a jet of water on to the surfaces. Do not permit any water to get on to the wheel-hub bearings, brakes, and carburettor. Where a hose is not at hand, soak the mud and then disperse it with plenty of clean water, using a sponge and pail.

After removing all dirt or mud, dry the enamelled surfaces with a chamois leather and afterwards polish them with soft dusters and some good wax polish or a proprietary polish such as "Autobrite." I, myself, am more or less a "fine-weather" rider, mainly because I hate cleaning a muddy machine. I do manage to keep it in almost "showroom" condition merely by rubbing over all parts with a slightly paraffin-damped cloth and then polishing with a dry duster. If a machine is very dirty, this method of cleaning is, of course, quite useless.

The Chromium Plating. Do not use any liquid metal polish or paste for cleaning purposes, as this will rub down the thin chromium surface. It is permissible, however, to use some good chromium cleaning compound occasionally. The correct method of removing tarnish (salt deposits) is to wipe over the surfaces regularly with a damp chamois leather and then polish with soft dusters. "Belco" is a good cleaning compound.

How to Reduce Tarnishing. During the damp winter months is it a good plan occasionally to wipe over all surfaces with a cloth soaked in a proprietary anti-tarnish preparation such as "Tekall," obtainable from accessory firms in pint and half-pint tins.

Check Nuts Regularly for Tightness. Apply spanners regularly to the various external nuts and bolts to ensure tightness, paying particular attention to the engine nuts and bolts, the nuts on the engine-mounting bolts, and the pipe unions. After the running-in period is completed, check over the external nuts and bolts regularly, say every 2,000 miles. After decarbonizing, check over the cylinder-head retaining nuts after a brief mileage.

Bantam Lubrication. Detailed instructions for the correct lubrication of 1948 and subsequent Bantams are given in Chapter 2, and the lubrication chart on page 21 explains at a glance when and where to lubricate the power unit and machine.

Carburettor Tuning and Maintenance. For full information on the Amal carburettor fitted to all Bantams, refer to Chapter 3.

Maintenance of Ignition System. Chapter 4 contains all essential maintenance advice concerning Wipac and Lucas flywheel generators, sparking plugs, and other components of the ignition systems provided on the 1948–70 Bantams.

The Ignition Timing. No alteration to the timing is normally permissible, but if there is any doubt about the timing being correct, it can readily be checked as described on page 51.

Loss of Compression. Provided that you keep your Bantam tank replenished with the correct petroil mixture (*see* page 17), it is extremely unlikely that you will experience any loss of compression (and consequent decline in power output) until a very big mileage has been covered. Ultimately, of course, some loss of compression will occur because of cylinder barrel and piston ring wear. It should be noted, however, that on D1, D3 and other Competition Bantams some loss of compression may occur at intervals of 3,000–5,000 miles because of poor seating of the decompressor valve (omitted on touring models) screwed into the cylinder head.

It is advisable each time the above are decarbonized to examine and clean the decompressor valve. With a screwdriver applied to the valve head, rotate the valve backwards and forwards. Some paraffin will help to clean carbon deposits off the valve seating. If absolutely necessary, apply a smear of fine-grade grinding paste to the valve face and gently grind the valve on to its seat, lifting the valve every few oscillations to turn it to a new position. It should in practice rarely be necessary to grind-in a decompressor valve, as it is only used for starting and stopping purposes, and is in no way analogous to an exhaust valve on a four-stroke engine.

DECARBONIZING, ETC.

Carbon deposits form slowly but surely inside the engine (on the piston crown, the inside of the combustion chamber, and the exhaust port) because of: (*a*) incomplete combustion of fuel, (*b*) the burning of oil deposited by the petroil mixture, and (*c*) the burning of some road dust.

The formation of excessive carbon deposits inside the engine soon becomes apparent because of the disconcerting symptoms which accompany them. For instance, a Bantam begins to tire readily and lacks its former youthful liveliness and power; it begins to "pink" under slight provocation (particularly when there is a sudden increase in load); the two-stroke engine becomes noticeably "rough" and begins to run erratically, with excessive four- and eight-stroking.

A decline in power output is especially pronounced when carbon commences to foul the exhaust port. Such fouling obstructs the free escape of the exhaust gases, and prevents proper scavenging of the cylinder, an essential pre-condition for the efficient transfer of the combustible mixture from the crankcase.

Decarbonizing is an extremely simple operation to perform on the Bantam, and to obtain consequently smooth and "peppy" running, it is advisable to decarbonize at regular intervals of approximately 2,500–3,000 miles.

Cylinder Head Removal Normally Sufficient. It is normally unnecessary, and indeed undesirable, to remove the cylinder barrel at each "decoke." Most of the carbon deposits (except slight deposits under the piston crown) can readily be removed when the exhaust pipe and cylinder head are taken off. Therefore defer removing the cylinder barrel until such time as it is reasonably desirable to inspect the piston rings, the piston and the underneath of the piston crown. If compression is bad, remove the barrel after removing the cylinder head.

Petrol Tank Removal Unnecessary. If it is intended to remove the cylinder head, but not the barrel, you need not touch the fuel tank. However, should you wish to remove the cylinder head *and* the cylinder barrel, you should first raise the tank slightly. This greatly facilitates the removal of the cylinder barrel from the four long studs which retain the barrel and head to the crankcase.

To raise the tank at the rear, first loosen the two bolts securing the tank to the steering head, and remove completely the longer bolt securing the rear of the tank to the frame. This bolt, by the way, carries the earth lead of the electrical system. See that the fuel tap is turned off, disconnect the fuel pipe from the float chamber, and then raise the tank about one inch.

Note that on many Bantams a plastic-type petrol pipe is used, the upper end of the pipe being clipped to the petrol-tap union. It is not advisable to disturb this end of the petrol pipe unnecessarily. Normally it is quite sufficient to disconnect the pipe by unscrewing the union nut situated on top of the carburettor float-chamber.

To Remove the Cylinder Head from Barrel. First remove the air filter which is retained on the carburettor intake either by a clip bolt or by being screwed on (according to model). In the case of the 1968 and subsequent models, disconnect the air-hose clip.

Unscrew the mixing-chamber cap and release the clip bolt securing the carburettor to the induction stub, or, in the case of the 1958–70 D5, D7, D10 and D14 models, release the two nuts securing the carburettor flange to the rear of the cylinder. Withdraw the carburettor, and at the same time pull out the throttle slide and (on 1966–70 models) the air slide, together with the tapered jet-needle. Tie these up carefully out of the way. Place the carburettor in a box or on a sheet of clean paper. It is essential that no dirt is permitted to enter the instrument.

With a C spanner Part No. 68-9462 unscrew the union nut from the front of the cylinder barrel. If this nut should be difficult to turn, apply a few drops of penetrating oil to the threaded portion of the barrel immediately above the nut. Allow some time to elapse to enable the oil to penetrate around the threads before applying force with the C spanner. Now disconnect the exhaust pipe, or remove the pipe and silencer (two nuts).

Disconnect the high-tension lead from the 14 mm sparking plug, and with a box spanner, unscrew and remove the plug and its washer. On Competition models also disconnect the cable from the decompressor lever at the cylinder-head connection. Now with the appropriate spanner, unscrew evenly and in a diagonal order the four nuts securing the cylinder head and barrel, and withdraw the head (*see* Fig. 40) from the long crankcase studs. Never attempt to prise of the head which is of light alloy (1954–70) and is easily damaged. No gasket is used for the head joint, this being of the metal-to-metal type.

Withdrawing Cylinder Barrel. As has already been mentioned opposite, it is not necessary to remove the cylinder barrel each time the engine is decarbonized. Having taken off the cylinder head, to remove the barrel (in order to examine the piston and rings), turn the engine over so that the piston is well down on its stroke, and then with *both* hands carefully withdraw the barrel.

On the Bantam models there is ample room for the cylinder barrel to clear the tops of the four long crankcase-studs, without fouling the tank if it has already been raised slightly (*see* page 90).

As the piston emerges from the mouth of the cylinder barrel, steady it with one hand. The light alloy deflectorless-type piston must never be allowed to fall sharply against the side of the connecting-rod, as this may damage or distort the piston skirt. The slightest distortion (not necessarily visible to the naked eye) can have a most detrimental effect upon engine efficiency. The piston is perhaps the most vital part of the engine, but the most vulnerable when exposed. Therefore always treat it with the greatest respect.

After removing the cylinder barrel, inspect the compressed paper washer provided between the crankcase top face and the cylinder barrel. This must be in perfect condition. If it is in any way damaged, it must immediately be renewed, otherwise some loss of crankcase compression may occur during downward piston strokes.

As soon as possible after removing the cylinder barrel, wrap a non-fluffy rag or duster round the upper portion of the connecting-rod so as to cover completely the crankcase mouth. This will not only protect the piston and connecting-rod from swaying about and being damaged, but also elimin-ate the risk of some foreign body (such as a nut) or dirt entering the crank-case. If a nut does get into the crankcase, fishing it out can be a most tiresome business, especially on a sunny day! Lay the cylinder barrel and head in a safe position on the bench or floor, and have a look at the piston skirt and the piston rings. Examine the latter closely.

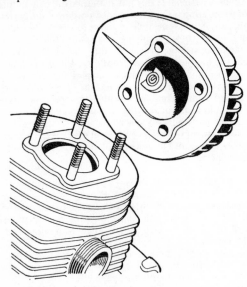

Fig. 40. Cylinder head removed

To Remove the Piston. The slightly domed die-cast piston, which, according to model, has either two or three plain rings, is secured to the small end of the connecting-rod by means of a fully-floating hollow gudgeon-pin secured in position by a pair of steel circlips (*see* Fig. 41).

It is seldom actually necessary to remove the piston from the connecting-rod, but when it is desired to make a close bench examination of the piston

Fig. 41.
The circlips

and rings, it is obviously advisable to remove the gudgeon-pin and take off the piston.

To remove the gudgeon-pin, first remove with a small pair of snipe-nosed pliers, or other suitable implement, the two steel circlips from the grooves in the piston bosses. After removal, scrap the circlips, as they may be distorted or have lost springiness. Now, holding the piston firmly with one hand (to prevent any bending stresses on the connecting-rod), tap out the gudgeon-pin from the opposite side.

The gudgeon-pin is a somewhat close fit in the piston bosses, and if it cannot readily be tapped out while holding the piston with one hand, the safest course is first to warm the piston by means of a rag soaked in hot water and wrung out. Alternatively, apply a hot electric iron to the top of the piston crown. This will cause the aluminium-alloy piston to expand more than the steel gudgeon-pin. It should then be possible to push or tap out the pin quite readily. Alternatively, press out the gudgeon-pin with a proprietary gudgeon-pin removal tool. On 1962–70 D7, D10, D14, and Bantam 175 engines be careful not to damage the needle rollers in the small-end bearing. As the gudgeon-pin emerges, note its position relatively to the piston bosses. Mark one end as it is desirable always to replace it in the same running position. Lay the piston on the bench, or other safe place, and cover up the crankcase mouth.

Mark the Piston. Immediately you remove the piston, it is advisable to scratch an "R" mark on the inside of the skirt to indicate which is the rear. There is no deflector (used on most earlier two-stroke engines) on the piston crown which can be utilized for identification purposes. The piston must always be replaced in exactly the same position as originally fitted, because: (a) it laps out the cylinder bore in a specific manner, depending upon various factors such as thrust, lubrication, etc.; (b) the arrangement of the piston rings and ports is designed for one piston only (see page 99).

Examining the Piston Rings. If you go to the trouble of removing the piston, consider also removing the piston rings. The rings are responsible for maintaining compression and must therefore be full of springiness and in good condition. Before removing the rings, however, make a careful visual inspection of the rings which are located in their grooves and prevented from rotating (and thus possibly fouling the ports) by means of pegs which engage the rings at the piston ring gaps.

If the rings have a uniformly smooth metallic surface over their entire peripheries and have ample springiness, as evidenced by the fact that their "free" gap is considerably greater than their closed gap (see page 97), the rings are doubtless in sound condition and are functioning well. The state of engine compression is generally a reliable guide to the condition of the rings.

Should the piston rings on visual examination show signs of having been subjected to excessive heat, as indicated by brown or dark patches, they must be removed and renewed. The same applies if the rings have become stuck in their grooves, causing gas leakage. In this case it is likely that the piston ring lands and skirt are also scorched. Gummed-up rings must, of course, be removed, and substantial carbon deposits must be scraped from both the rings and their grooves.

If the piston rings appear to be in thoroughly good condition and carbon deposits are not appreciable, it is generally best not to disturb the rings. To remove them unnecessarily is bad practice and can cause temporary loss of compression without achieving any positive results. But if the condition of the rings is genuinely in doubt, remove them so that they and their grooves in the piston can be closely inspected.

Note that on the Bantam two-stroke engine excessive piston ring wear is most likely to be accompanied by a definite rise in petroil consumption, and if the wear is very pronounced some piston slap will probably be noticed, and possibly a peculiar sound known as "two-stroke rattle."

To Remove the Piston Rings. The compression rings fitted to the Bantam engine are made of cast iron and are of small section. They are therefore very brittle and easily broken if care is not taken during ring removal. The safest and most convenient method of removing (and fitting) the piston rings is indicated in Fig. 42. Insert three strips of sheet metal about 2 in. long and about ⅜ in. wide under the rings. Then gently ease the compression rings off, starting with the top ring. Before commencing to ease each ring

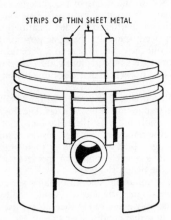

STRIPS OF THIN SHEET METAL

Fig. 42. The safest way to remove piston rings

It is advisable to employ this method also when fitting new rings or replacing the old ones. The two-stroke piston has no deflector, and the two plain compression rings are pegged. Recent D7 and D10 engines have three piston rings fitted, including a scraper ring, but the D14 and Bantam 175 engines reverted to two compression rings

off, see that its ends are clear of the locating peg in the piston groove. It is desirable, though not essential, to replace a serviceable ring in its original groove. Therefore lay the rings aside in such a manner that they can be identified on assembly.

When removing the rings, be particularly careful to avoid scratching or otherwise damaging the land between the rings and the land above the top ring. Any scoring here is most detrimental to engine efficiency. Should the rings be badly gummed-up by sticky carbon deposits, it is advisable to immerse the piston in a paraffin bath for about 20 minutes in order to soften the carbon. In extreme cases it may be necessary to remove the piston rings with a proprietary removal tool, or perhaps even to snap the rings off.

Should a slight piston seizure ever occur (generally caused by driving the engine too hard under unfavourable circumstances), it is probable that some smearing of the aluminium alloy at the edges of the lands will prevent the rings from springing out and thereby cause serious loss of engine compression. If the smearing is very bad, accompanied by scoring, the piston will have to be scrapped. If, on the other hand, the smearing is very slight, an expert mechanic can remove the barest amount of smeared metal with a very fine file and restore the piston and rings to serviceable condition.

Removing the Carbon Deposits. For scraping off carbon deposits from the piston, cylinder head, etc., it is advisable to use a blunt screwdriver or a proprietary scraper. For cleaning piston-ring grooves you can make up a suitable scraper by fitting a handle to a broken piece of piston ring ground at one end; alternatively you can obtain a proprietary piston-ring groove scraper.

Thorough decarbonizing is always worthwhile because carbon forms more slowly on smooth, clean surfaces. Where carbon deposits are found to be heavy, the application of a little paraffin will generally facilitate decarbonizing.

If removal of the cylinder head only has been effected, thoroughly scrape all carbon deposits from the piston crown, the combustion chamber walls, and the exhaust port of the cylinder barrel.

When removing carbon from the piston crown, be careful not to scratch deeply the aluminium-alloy surface and (except where the piston has been removed) do not use any abrasive such as emery cloth. If any abrasive particles get between the piston and the cylinder bore, they can cause most serious scoring of the highly polished cylinder barrel, and perhaps ruin the barrel. After decarbonizing the piston crown, wipe it with an oily rag to remove all loose particles.

Lay the cylinder head on the bench and chip off all carbon deposits from the combustion-chamber walls. The Bantam cylinder head (1954–70 models) is of aluminium alloy, and great care must be taken not to scratch it deeply with the decarbonizing tool. Do not forget to clean up the sparking plug hole, and when you have thoroughly decarbonized the combustion chamber wipe it clean with an oily rag.

The heaviest carbon deposits generally accumulate in the exhaust port and it is these deposits which cause considerable loss of power and a tendency for four-stroking to occur. When the exhaust pipe has been removed it is a simple matter to scrape off all carbon deposits from the port, but be very careful not to allow the scraper to slip inside the cylinder barrel and damage the bore surfaces.

If the cylinder barrel is removed as well as the cylinder head, also inspect closely the single inlet and twin tangential transfer ports for signs of carbon deposits. Until a considerable mileage has been covered, however, these deposits are unlikely to be heavy. But remove all existing deposits and afterwards wipe the cylinder bore and the inlet, exhaust, and transfer ports absolutely clean.

Where the piston has been removed and the rings taken off as previously described, remove any slight carbon deposits which may be present on the inside of the piston, but on no account touch the outside of the piston skirt. Clean the ring grooves very thoroughly, but be careful not to damage the sides of the grooves or the locating pegs. On a three-ring piston see that all carbon is removed from the slot at the bottom of the scraper ring groove. Also clean the backs of the piston rings and remove all carbon from the ends of each ring.

Cleaning the Silencer. If the silencer becomes badly choked up with carbon, some overheating, loss or power, and four stroking may occur due to excessive back pressure. On 1954–66 Model D1, D3, D7 and D7D/L Bantams the silencer has a detachable end cap and baffle, and the silencer can readily be taken apart and thoroughly cleaned. On 1948–53 models however, the silencer cannot be dismantled, and the best way to clean it effectively is to immerse the silencer in a caustic-soda solution of moderate strength. The caustic soda is, of course, corrosive, so keep it away from your hands and the chromium plating. Afterwards swill out the silencer thoroughly with water.

The 1954–63 silencer with detachable end-cap secured by a single central nut inside the exhaust opening can be dismantled as follows. Remove the nut and take off the cap and the internal baffle for thorough cleaning. When replacing the baffle unit, see that the copper sealing-ring is positioned before replacing the end cap. Replace the two plain washers and one spring washer on the stud before you tighten the central locking nut (1, Fig. 43).

The 1964–7 D7, D10 Bantams have a silencer provided with a detachable end-cap different from that shown in Fig. 43 and the internal baffles are not detachable. To clean the silencer remove the single nut and withdraw the end-cap. Then remove all carbon deposits from the cap and the baffles. To dissolve the carbon, if found difficult to remove, use a caustic soda solution. Before fitting the end-cap see that the copper sealing ring is replaced. Before replacing and tightening the nut securing the end-cap do

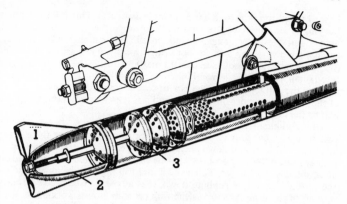

Fig. 43. The Bantam silencer with detachable end-cap and baffle
(1954–63)

After removing the nut 1, the end-cap 2 can be removed and the baffle 3 withdrawn for cleaning

(By courtesy of "Motor Cycling")

not forget to replace the plain washer and spring washer on the locating stud.

The 1968–70 D14 silencers are of different internal construction, those for the 1968 models containing spiral disc baffles mounted on a central tube, which can be withdrawn for cleaning purposes. Later models were of tubular construction and can be completely dismantled in the same way. Cleaning notes are as for the D7 models.

Fitting the Piston Rings. Indications that piston-ring renewal is called for have already been described on page 93. It is assumed that the piston-ring grooves have been thoroughly cleaned, the old rings also if these are found to be in serviceable condition and their gaps are within the permissible limits (*see* below). To replace the piston rings, use the method shown in Fig. 42, after first smearing a little engine oil on the rings and grooves. Fit the *bottom* ring first.

If the old rings are no longer serviceable, but the piston itself shows no signs of abnormal wear and is in sound condition, fit a new set of genuine B.S.A. Bantam rings. Piston rings of genuine B.S.A. manufacture are correctly gapped for use and have ample clearance for the locating pegs. Such may not be the case, however, if rings other than those of B.S.A. manufacture are used, and here it is essential to check the ring gaps, the fit of the rings in their grooves, and the clearances for the locating pegs.

To check the working gap of each piston ring, first insert the ring into the bore of the cylinder barrel and push it forward by pressing on it with the base of the piston skirt (or a bar of suitable diameter). This will ensure that the ring is absolutely square with the bore when the ring gap is checked with a suitable feeler gauge. To obtain efficient running on a Bantam engine, the piston ring gap (for both rings) must not be less than 0·009 in. (0·2 mm) and should not exceed 0·013 in. (0·3 mm). If the piston-ring gap is too small, remove a little metal from one end of the ring with a file, so as to increase the gap to 0·009 in. The gap, of course, gradually increases as wear of the ring and cylinder bore occurs, and it is therefore advisable to set the gap to the lowest permissible limit.

After checking that the piston-ring gap is correct, insert the ring in the piston-ring groove and verify that it is free to move without there being any appreciable up and down play. If the ring is a tight fit, rub down carefully *one* side of the ring on a sheet of fine emery cloth which must be laid on an absolutely flat surface. To ensure a uniform pressure being exerted on the piston ring during rubbing down, it is advisable to employ a rotary motion of the arm. As soon as the ring becomes a nice working fit in its groove (0·002 in.), clean the ring prior to fitting it.

It is essential to see that sufficient clearance exists between the inner portion of the piston-ring gap and the small locating peg in the piston ring groove. With finger pressure applied to the ring, fitted in its groove, close up the ring until the gap is reduced to nil, in which case there is obviously sufficient clearance at the peg. If it is impossible to reduce the gap to nil, the steps of the ring must be fouling the peg, and it is necessary to file the steps very carefully and lightly, using a very smooth file.

Testing the Connecting-rod Bearings. When you have occasion to withdraw both the cylinder head and the cylinder barrel, it is worth while taking the opportunity of checking the connecting-rod bearings for excessive wear. If very considerable wear has occurred you will probably have already noted in the case of the small-end bearing, a metallic "tinkling" noise or, in the case of the big-end bearing, a dull knock or rattling sound. The Bantam connecting-rod bearings (*see* Fig. 44), however, are of the heavy duty type and of generous proportions.

Provided that you are reasonably careful in handling your Bantam and are not neglectful in regard to petroil lubrication, you will find it possible to cover a very big mileage without having to renew either of the connecting rod bearings. Bearing renewal is a job which should be entrusted only to a really competent repairer or agent, as it requires considerable skill and special facilities, including the use of certain B.S.A. service tools. If the big-end bearing is in poor shape, the renewal of the roller bearing will involve the splitting of the flywheel assembly, an operation not likely to be undertaken with success by the inexperienced.

A convenient method of checking the small-end bearing for wear is to replace the gudgeon-pin in the small end bush and feel its fit by attempting to "rock" it in the bush. Although the gudgeon-pin must be able to rotate with perfect freedom, there should be no appreciable "rock" present.

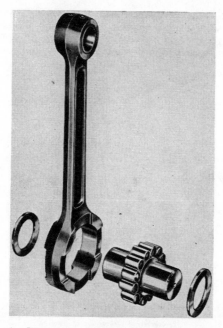

Fig. 44. The Bantam connecting-rod and sturdy big-end roller
bearing (Models D1, D3)

To check the big-end bearing for wear, rotate the Bantam engine so that
the single-row roller bearing is at the top of its movement, i.e. at T.D.C.
(top dead centre), and then by gripping the connecting-rod with both
hands and trying gently but firmly to pull and push the connecting-rod
vertically, note whether there is any appreciable play present. None should
exist, but some end movement is permissible and necessary. Be careful not
to confuse end play with vertical play. If you do detect some vertical play
but are not sufficiently experienced to determine whether it is sufficient
to justify bearing renewal, it is best to obtain the opinion of an expert
mechanic.

To Replace the Piston. It is assumed that the piston rings have been fitted,
and that the piston itself is thoroughly clean internally and externally. Now
offer up the piston to the small-end of the connecting-rod. When doing this
make absolutely sure that the piston is replaced the correct way round (*see*
page 93), with the two ring gaps to the *rear* in the case of Model D1 engines

and to the *front* on all other Bantam engines with extra wide ports; it is hence vitally important that the ring gaps face to the front. Next oil the gudgeon-pin and replace it in its *original position*. Insert it into the piston bosses and small-end bush after first fitting one of the two *new* circlips.

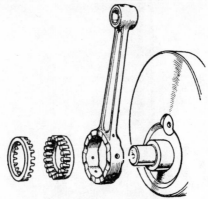

Fig. 45. Connecting-rod, caged rollers (Models D5, D7, D10, and Bantam 175)

Applies also to 1959–63 Model D1. On D7, D10, D14, and Bantam 175 engines a needle roller race is provided instead of a phosphor bronze bush for the small-end
(By courtesy of "Motor Cycle," London)

When tapping the gudgeon-pin home with a soft-metal drift and hammer, be very careful to support the piston firmly on the opposite side; if the pin is a very obstinate fit, first warm the piston by immersing it in hot water or by wrapping round it a rag soaked in hot water and wrung out. Alternatively, press the gudgeon-pin home with a suitable proprietary gudgeon-pin removal tool. See that the crankcase mouth is covered.

After tapping or pressing the gudgeon-pin until it abuts the circlip already fitted, carefully fit the second *new* circlip. When fitting it with a small pair of snipe-nosed pliers, squeeze the circlip ends together and employ a rotary motion of the hand to ensure that the circlip beds down snugly into the piston-boss groove. Remember that should a circlip spring out while the engine is running, the cylinder bore may easily be spoiled beyond repair; deep scores may be caused.

Pending the replacement of the cylinder barrel and cylinder head, cover up the piston as well as the crankcase mouth with a clean cloth.

Replacing the Cylinder Barrel and Head. Before replacing the cylinder barrel, wipe the cylinder bore thoroughly clean with a soft rag and some clean paraffin, and be very careful not to scratch its glossy surface. Check that the cylinder barrel spigot for the crankcase face, and the crankcase face itself, are absolutely clean. Also verify that the cylinder-base washer is in perfect condition. Should this compressed-paper washer be in any way damaged, renew it immediately and make sure that the washer referred to is correctly positioned. It is a good plan to smear some grease on both sides of the washer before fitting it to the crankcase face.

Smear some clean engine oil liberally on the outside of the piston and the inside of the cylinder barrel (i.e. the bore) and turn the engine over slowly until the piston is at or near the bottom of its stroke. Now replace the cylinder barrel over the piston and the four crankcase studs, carefully easing the piston rings with the fingers into the mouth of the cylinder barrel as the latter descends. Both rings must enter the bore readily without the necessity for using any force. It will be of considerable assistance in making a satisfactory job of this operation if a "slipper"—B.S.A. Service Tool 61–5051—is used to compress the rings while the piston is entering the cylinder bore. It is also important when lowering the cylinder barrel to make sure that it beds down properly on to the cylinder-base washer.

As soon as you have replaced the cylinder barrel, fit the head on the upper face of the barrel. No gasket is required, but the two contacting faces must be absolutely clean. Then replace the washers and nuts on the four holding-down studs. To avoid any risk of distorting the cylinder head, be most careful to tighten the four nuts evenly and in a diagonal order.

Final Assembly. Do this in the reverse order of dismantling. Replace the sparking plug (assumed to have been thoroughly cleaned and checked for gap), including the washer which must be in perfect condition and not flattened. Tighten the plug finger-tight first, and then firmly with a box-spanner. Reconnect the HT lead to the plug and make sure that its terminal connection is secure. On Competition models also reconnect the decompressor-valve operating cable to the decompressor unit screwed into the cylinder head.

Reposition the exhaust pipe and silencer (if previously completely re-moved), and with a mallet tap the exhaust pipe so that its end goes home into the exhaust port. Do not omit the gas-sealing ring. When doing this it is advisable to interpose a rag to prevent the risk of denting the pipe, and to apply the taps at several different points. On some engines a sharp blow with the closed fist may push the pipe home. Then with the C spanner securely tighten the union ring-nut which secures the pipe to the exhaust port of the cylinder barrel. The clip which secures the rear end of the pipe (and the silencer) can now be tightened down.

Replace the carburettor on the induction stub or flange (according to model). Before tightening the clip, check that the mixture chamber is truly vertical. Now insert the throttle slide, air slide (1966–70) and the tapered jet-needle. Afterwards replace the mixing-chamber cap, and with the twist-grip check that the throttle slide works freely.

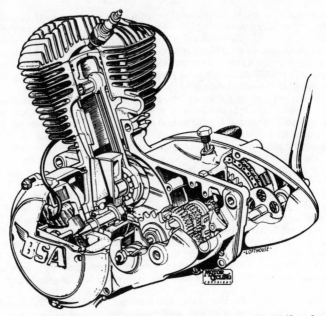

Fig. 46. Partly cut-away and sectioned view of assembled 148 cm³ "Bantam Major" power unit

The engine shown has Wipac direct-ignition. Apart from the bore being increased from 52 mm to 57 mm, and the use of a light-alloy cylinder head and deeper cylinder finning, this engine is almost identical to the 123 cm³ Bantam engines which have a stroke of 58 mm.
(By courtesy of "Motor Cycling")

If you have previously removed the cylinder barrel as well as the cylinder head, lower the petrol tank into its normal position at the rear and fit the long bolt securing this part of the tank to the frame. Before inserting this bolt, pass it through the earth connection tag attached to the electrical-system harness. To ensure good electrical contact, make certain that the tag is not dirty or corroded. Finally, with the appropriate spanners, firmly tighten the long rear bolt and the two shorter bolts securing the forward end of the tank to the steering head. Also reconnect the fuel pipe to the tank union. When tightening the fuel pipe union-nut, do not omit to hold the top hexagon with a spanner, otherwise you may strain the joint at the tank.

To Remove the Bantam Power Unit. Complete removal of the power unit is advisable for all work other than normal maintenance, including decarbonizing. The Bantam unit can readily be taken out of the loop frame. To do this this, remove the air filter and then the carburettor as explained on page 90, and then the decompressor cable (on Competition models), and the clutch cable. Also disconnect the fuel pipe, and the electrical lead from the flywheel generator. Next, with the "C" spanner unscrew the exhaust pipe union-nut (*see* page 91) and disconnect the exhaust pipe from the exhaust port. Remove the pipe and silencer together.

Disconnect the secondary chain and remove the chain and its guard. Now remove the nuts from the four bolts (two at the front of the crankcase, and two at the rear, one of these being below the engine) which secure the power unit to the frame members. Pull the bolts away, or if necessary tap them out with a suitable drift. Then carefully withdraw the complete Bantam power unit from the frame.

MAINTENANCE OF MOTOR-CYCLE PARTS

Do not be very conscientious in regard to engine maintenance, and at the same time neglect the motor-cycle parts. Proper and regular maintenance of the motor-cycle itself is really most important, and this applies particularly to the transmission, responsible for transmitting power from the engine to the road wheels. It always pays to keep down friction and wear of *all* moving parts to the absolute minimum, and to preserve that "showroom" appearance for as long as possible.

Items Needed for Maintenance. These are all included in the appropriate section on page 26. It is a simple matter to pick out those items not concerned with engine maintenance.

Tools Required. A comprehensive tool kit, plus a chain rivet extractor (not often needed), plus the B.S.A. service tool shown in Fig. 57, is normally sufficient for all routine maintenance, stripping-down, and assembly. If you wish to undertake repair work as well as maintenance, you will require a bench and some additional tools (*see* page 87).

Riding Tactics and Tyre Wear. These are very closely associated. Some riders are constantly paying heavy bills for tyres. Others obtain phenomenal mileages before tyre renewal becomes necessary. Above all, see that the tyre pressures are always maintained correctly and that the wheels are in true alignment.

Check the Tyre Pressures Weekly. It is just not good enough to use the old method of testing pressures by kicking the tyres before a run! Over-inflation causes discomfort, a tendency for skidding, vibration, strains the covers, and can result in a sudden concussion burst if a road irregularity is hit at speed. Under-inflation induces a proneness for tyre creep, rolling, instability of steering, and eventual cracking of the covers. Always check the tyre pressures weekly[1] with a suitable pressure gauge such as the Dunlop pencil-type No. 6, the Romac, the Holdtite, or the Schrader No. 7750 gauge. Keep the valve caps screwed down firmly, as slight leakage often occurs at the valves. Remove the valve "inners" annually.

The correct tyre-inflation pressures for 1948–70 solo Bantam models are given in Table II and these recommendations should be strictly adhered to,

Table II
CORRECT TYRE PRESSURES (IN LB PER SQ IN.) FOR 1948–70
B.S.A. BANTAMS (SOLO)

Model	D1	D3, D5	D7, D10, D14, Bantam 175
Front	16	16	17
Rear (Touring)	22	24	22
Rear (Competition)	16	16	—

except when a pillion passenger or heavy luggage is carried, in which case the pressure for the *rear* tyre should be increased by 5–10 lb per sq in., according to the extra load carried. Most riders increase the rear-tyre pressure by about 7 lb per sq in. when a medium-weight pillion passenger is carried.

Note that the tyre pressure recommendations given in Table II are correct for a solo rider weighing not more than 140 lb (10 stone). Should you be heavier than 140 lb, or carry a pillion passenger and/or heavy luggage, strictly speaking, the tyre pressures should be increased by one lb per sq in. for every 28 lb increase (front tyre), or 14 lb increase (rear tyre); or in accordance with Table III.

Table III
MINIMUM TYRE PRESSURES FOR SPECIFIC LOADS

Nominal tyre section (in.)	Inflation Pressures (lb per sq in.)					
	16	18	20	24	28	32
	Load per Tyre (lb)					
2·75	140	160	180	210	250	280
3·25	200	240	280	350	400	440
3·00	160	180	200	240	300	350

[1] Natural rubber tubes are porous, and a loss in pressure of 2–4 lb per sq in. weekly is normal (whether a machine is ridden or left standing). With the "Butyl" tubes (now supplied by the Dunlop Co. Ltd.) there is little porosity and the tyre pressures remain constant for an appreciable time.

Where an abnormal load is carried, the technically correct method of deciding the appropriate inflation pressures is to ride your Bantam to the nearest weighbridge (provided at most large railway stations and transport depots) and check individually the fully laden weight (with pillion passenger *seated*) on the front and rear tyre. Then for the appropriate inflation pressures, consult Table III.

Removing Inner Tube. On the Bantam the mudguards are somewhat heavily valanced and if a puncture occurs (even if its exact position is known), it is generally advisable to remove the wheel to avoid the risk of dirtying or damaging the tube when removing it from the cover. Wheel removal is described on pages 115, 116.

To remove one side of the cover prior to complete or partial withdrawal of the tube, first unscrew the valve cap and remove the valve core to ensure complete deflation of the tyre. Lay these two parts on the bench or table so that no dirt or grit can enter them.

Next press *both* wire beads off their seats. Insert a tyre lever *close to the valve stem*, and while pulling on this tyre lever, press the bead diametrically opposite into the well of the rim. Now insert a second tyre lever close to the first one, and lever the bead over the flange of the rim. When doing this, hold the removed portion of the bead with the first lever. Then remove one tyre lever and reinsert it a little farther away from the first one. Continue right round the bead in stages (about three inches apart) until the whole of the bead is removed. You can now push in the valve stem and withdraw the tube.

Repairing a Puncture. If the precise position of the puncture is unknown, submerge the inflated tube in water and watch for tell-tale air bubbles. Clean the tube in the vicinity of the puncture with some fine sand-paper and rub off all dust.

Select a suitable patch (not too small), preferably of the autovulcanizing type such as the "Vulcafix," and remove its linen backing. If rubber solution is not used, rub the prepared face of the patch with a cloth moistened in petrol and transfer the brown deposit on the cloth to the tube, around the puncture. Repeat this operation and allow the patch and transferred deposit to dry for one minute. If solution is used, apply it *to the tube only* and allow it to become "tacky." Now affix the patch, using slight pressure, particularly at the edges, and apply a little french chalk.

Replacing Tube and Cover. Before replacing the tube in the cover, inflate the tube just enough to round it out without causing it to stretch. This will reduce any tendency for twisting or for the tube to be nipped during the application of the tyre levers.

Fit the tube (see that it is not twisted and beds down snugly) and insert the valve stem through the hole in the wheel rim. At this stage screw down the knurled ring-nut only about half an inch. It is assumed that the wheel is horizontal; push the lower bead well down into the well of the rim *close to the valve*. Now start to press the upper bead home with the hands, commencing diametrically opposite to the valve. Use hand pressure except for the last portion of the cover (close to the valve), where the use of tyre levers (*see* Fig. 47) is generally called for. Push the valve stem into the

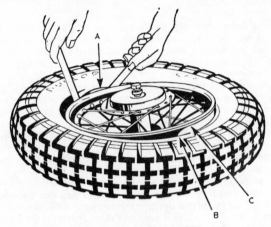

Fig. 47. Completing replacement of one side of the cover after inserting the inner tube

Always remember that wired-type beads cannot stretch. Therefore before attempting to lever the cover at A over the wheel rim, you must push the cover bead at B off the shoulder C down into the well of the rim

cover and then pull it down firmly by tightening the knurled ring-nut. Replace the valve core and pump up the tyre to the correct inflation pressure (*see* page 104), "thumbing" the cover at intervals to ensure that the beads are seating squarely all round. Finally, screw home the valve cap and replace the front or rear wheel in the motor-cycle (*see* page 116).

Correct Tyre Sizes. 2·75 × 19 tyres are required for the front and rear wheels of all Touring Bantams (Models D1 and D3), and for the *front* wheel of all Competition Bantams (Models D1 and D3). With 1958–70 Models D5, D7, D10, D14, and Bantam 175, however, the correct tyre size for the front and rear wheel is 3·00 × 18.

The Lighting Equipment. For full maintenance instructions concerning the Wipac and Lucas flywheel generators, batteries, and lamps, *see* Chapter 5. Wiring diagrams are given on pages 77–84 for the various Bantam models fitted with different types of lighting equipment.

Cleaning the Machine. For advice on cleaning the enamelled and chromium-plated motor-cycle parts, *see* page 88.

Bantam Lubrication. The correct lubrication of the various motor-cycle parts (excluding engine lubrication), is dealt with in detail on pages 20–5 in Chapter 2. Carefully observe items, 3, 4 and 7–20 on the lubrication chart given on page 21.

Check Nuts and Bolts for Tightness. After completing about 250 miles on a new machine, and subsequently about every 2,000 miles, check over the various nuts and bolts for tightness, paying special attention to the wheel-spindle nuts and the nuts and bolts on the forks. Do not overlook (on battery-lighting models) the battery-strap securing-bolt. Occasionally this slackens off, causing the battery to move about on the battery carrier. The battey should not be able to move, but avoid over-tightening the strap securing-bolt (two bolts fitted on D3, D5, D7 and D7D/L). On D10, D14, and Bantam 175 models (1967–70), the battery is retained by a "toggle-action" wire clamp which must be released before the battery can be removed.

The Front Forks (D1, D3, D5). Besides an occasional check for tightness of the nuts and bolts, and the weekly application of the grease gun to the fork nipples (*see* page 23), no maintenance is necessary. The forks have internal compression springs and (on 1951–9 Competition models) rubber shock-absorbers fitted inside the springs. No hydraulic damping, requiring topping-up of the fork legs, and no adjustment are provided.

Concertina-type rubber or plastic (March, 1952, onwards) gaiters (*A*, Fig. 50) are fitted to the lower ends of the fork legs to prevent the entry of dust or dirt into the moving parts. It is a good plan about every 3,000 miles, or when decarbonizing, to remove both gaiters and carefully clean and grease the sliding members of the fork legs. Never allow them to become dry or rusty. To remove 1948–53 gaiters it is first necessary to detach the spring-wire circlips which secure their upper and lower ends to the fork legs. The gaiters can then be taken off the legs. Be careful to fit all four circlips properly when replacing the gaiters. If a gaiter becomes cracked or damaged, it is advisable to renew it at the first opportunity. On 1954–63 Bantams the protective gaiters are a *push fit* on the tubes of the front fork.

It is rare for the maximum fork travel (normally 3¾ in.) to become increased because of weakening of the internal springs. But if fork movement becomes excessive, the forks should be stripped-down and the springs and oil seals examined and if necessary renewed. At the same time the phosphor-bronze bushes inside the fork legs should be inspected. If worn, the bushes should also be renewed. Note that on Bantams of vintage prior to May, 1951, the bushes are *fixed* to the outer fork-legs and the outer legs complete must be renewed if serious bush wear has occurred. Trouble with the telescopic front forks, however, is so infrequent and develops so slowly that I do not feel justified in including in this maintenance handbook detailed instructions for stripping-down the forks and reassembling them. If you do have occasion to undertake this work, I would refer you to B.S.A. Service Sheet No. 509 which contains the appropriate instructions.

The Front Forks (Models D7, D10, D14, and Bantam 175). No grease nipples are provided on the telescopic fork legs. The only maintenance normally necessary is the occasional renewal of the oil, the necessity for which is indicated by excessive fork movement. The procedure for renewing the oil and suitable types of oil to use are dealt with on page 23.

Rear Suspension Units. Rear suspension was introduced on B.S.A. Bantams as extra equipment in September, 1949. No maintenance of D1 and D3 units is required except 1,000 mile application of the grease gun to the nipples provided for lubrication (*see* page 24), and no adjustment is provided. If after very many thousands of miles, the maximum movement of the plungers (normally $2\frac{1}{4}$ in.) becomes excessive (although this is rare) because of weakening of the internal springs, it is advisable to dismantle each rear-suspension unit as described on page 121 and renew the two springs. The bushes in the sliding member should also be inspected at the same time for wear. Should they require to be renewed, you will have to replace the tube and bushes.

On Models D5, D7, D10, D14, and Bantam 175 swinging-arm type rear suspension is provided. The two suspension units each comprise a telescopic damper unit and a completely enclosed coil spring (exposed on later models). The hydraulic dampers are sealed during manufacture and require no maintenance. If trouble occurs, the damper units should be removed and renewed. Removal from the frame entails only the withdrawal of the upper pivot bolts and the bottom retaining nuts. The swinging arm pivot has grease nipples and these should not be overlooked (*see* page 24).

Steering Head Adjustment (Preliminaries). First raise the front wheel of your Bantam well clear of the ground. Place the machine on its central stand and then apply some weight to the saddle or dualseat so as to tilt the front wheel upwards. If play is felt on attempting to push the fork legs to and fro, adjust the steering head. First lessen the pinch bolt nut *C* (Fig. 48). Where a bulb horn is fitted, unscrew the horn and remove the steering-head dust cover so as to expose the lock-nut and the adjuster nut. If a bulb horn is not provided, unscrew the central plug, and on 1948–63 models remove the washer and dust cover.

To Adjust Steering Head (Model D1). After attending to the above preliminaries, loosen the small nut on the clip stud on each front-fork leg. Both of these nuts are readily accessible. On more recent models slacken the clip bolt on each fork leg below the lamp. You must, of course, first loosen the outer nuts securing the headlamp brackets, except on 1954–63 models

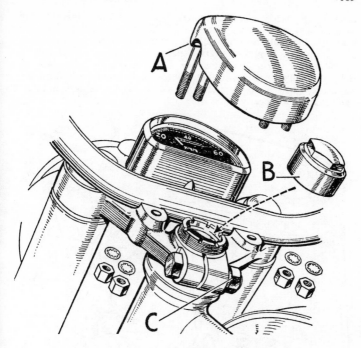

Fig. 48. Steering-head adjustment (Models D3, D5)

(By courtesy of "Motor Cycle," London)

having the headlamp brackets integral with the forks. The bottom yokes are now free to take up new positions when the head adjustment is made.

Slacken the lock-nut and tighten the adjuster nut situated beneath it until all steering head slackness has been eliminated. But avoid over-tightening the adjuster, otherwise the steering will become stiff and damage may be caused to the ball races. After the correct adjustment is obtained, tighten the lock-nut firmly, and also retighten the pinch-bolt nut *C* and the two clip nuts.

In the event of your removing both the lock-nut and the adjuster nut beneath it, make sure that on replacement the *thicker* adjuster nut is fitted first with its *recess downwards*.

To Adjust the Steering Head (Models D3, D5). Referring to Fig. 48, having dealt with the preliminaries (*see* page 108), remove the aluminium cover *A* which holds the handlebar bend in position, by unscrewing the four nuts beneath. This exposes the steering head lock-nut *B*; remove this nut. Now with a flat piece of metal applied to the adjuster-sleeve slots (the sleeve is below the lock-nut), turn the adjuster sleeve until all steering head slackness disappears. To prevent steering stiffness or damage to the ball races be careful not to over-tighten the sleeve. After the adjustment is made, re-tighten the nut *C* on the pinch-bolt, tighten the lock-nut above the adjuster sleeve, and replace the aluminium cover, being careful to align the handlebar bend properly.

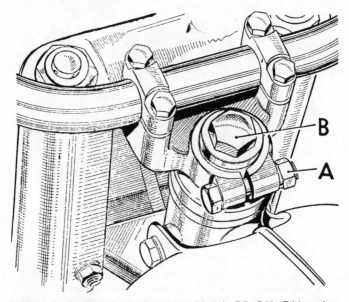

Fig. 49. Steering head adjustment (Models D7, D10, D14, and Bantam 175)

Steering Head Adjustment (Models D7, D10, D14, and Bantam 175). To take up any existing play first slacken the clip bolt on each fork leg below the headlamp or lamp nacelle (1964 onwards) to enable the bottom yoke to be free to take up a new position. Then, referring to Fig. 49, slacken the nut *A* on the steering head clip bolt and tighten the adjuster nut *B* until all slackness is taken up. Be careful not to over-tighten nut *B*, otherwise stiffness in the steering will occur and this may damage the ball races. Finally, firmly tighten nut *A* and the clip bolt on each fork leg so as to secure the bottom yoke.

Handlebars, Footrests. The footrests are adjustable only on Competition, D7 models (*see* page 4). Handlebars: *see* page 3.

Keep the Brakes Effective. To obtain powerful braking, it is desirable to keep both brakes adjusted so that with the brake pedal and lever released, the brake shoe linings almost make contact with the insides of the brake-drums. But both wheels must always be able to spin freely without any brake friction when the brakes are off.

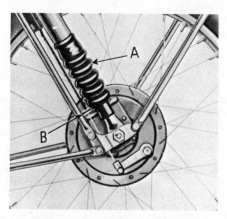

Fig. 50. Showing finger adjustment of front brake,
and the fork gaiters (D1, D3, D5)

The friction linings riveted to the brake shoes gradually wear, thereby reducing the effective brake leverage, and a compensating adjustment must therefore occasionally be made by taking up slackness in the hand or foot control. On all 1948 and subsequent Bantams, finger adjustment is provided for both brakes.

To effect an adjustment of the front brake, turn as required the knurled adjuster-nut located at the cable stop as shown at *B* in Fig. 50. To adjust the rear brake, screw the knurled adjuster-nut shown at *C* in Fig. 53 along the rear-brake rod as required.

The Brake Linings. When repeated finger-adjustments have been made to both brakes, the brake cam-operating levers eventually assume positions where their leverage is poor. In such circumstances the only satisfactory course to take is to remove the brake shoes for replacement. If you wish to reline the shoes yourself, you are referred to B.S.A. Service Sheet No. 611.

If excessive lubrication of the wheel hubs causes grease to get on the

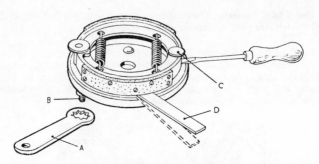

Fig. 51. Removing the brake shoes

brake linings and reduces stopping power, appreciably, it is wise to remove the brake shoes immediately and reline them or fit replacement shoes.

Harshness in brake action can often be remedied by filing down each brake lining for about one inch from each end. Note that new brake linings have rivet holes already drilled. The shoes themselves have no adjustment.

To Remove the Brake Shoes. The procedure is the same for front and rear brakes, the cover plates and shoes being similar in construction. First remove the wheel (*see* page 115), then unscrew the lock-nut on the wheel spindle, and the nut retaining the brake drum cover-plate. Withdraw the cover-plate and inspect the two shoes. Unless the brake linings are seriously worn and require to be renewed, it is not advisable to disturb the brake shoes.

Referring to Fig. 51, to remove the shoes from the brake cover-plate, first remove the brake operating-lever *A* from the serrations on the cam shaft *B*, and gently tap in the shaft until the cam plate clears the shoes. Now insert a screwdriver as shown between the shoe ends adjacent to the fulcrum pin *C*, and turn the screwdriver. Then place a small lever *D* between one shoe and the cover-plate, and prise the brake shoe upwards until you release the spring pressure. You can now withdraw the two shoes from the cover-plate.

The Non-adjustable Primary Chain. The primary chain (*see* Fig. 52) is sturdy (⅜ in. pitch) and it runs in short fixed centres in an oil-bath. Thus wear occurs very slowly indeed, and re-tensioning is neither necessary nor provided for. Only at very long intervals is chain renewal called for. It is, however, advisable to inspect the chain after covering many thousands of miles.

To inspect the primary chain, you must first take off the chaincase cover (*see* Fig. 7) after removing the foot gear-change and kick-starter levers.

Fig. 52. Showing the non-adjustable primary chain, and the clutch

The Bantam is one of the few machines with the primary transmission on the off side

These two levers are both located on their shafts by means of splines and secured by the pinch-bolts *C* and *B* (Fig. 7). Now remove the five cheese-headed screws *D* (Fig. 7) securing the cover, and carefully ease the cover off the primary drive chain-case. Do not attempt to prise it off. Then with the fingers check the tension of the primary chain in the centre of the lower chain run, with the chain in its tightest position. The total whip should be approximately ⅜ in. (1 cm), and the maximum permissible up-and-down movement is about ¾ in. (2 cm). When the total movement reaches the specified maximum limit, it is generally time to remove the connecting link, take off the chain, and fit a new one. Make sure that the spring link is correctly replaced (*see* page 114).

To Re-tension the Secondary Chain. The ½ in. pitch secondary chain, being of considerable length and protected only by a top run chain-guard instead of an oil-bath, naturally stretches far more quickly than does the primary chain. It is therefore advisable to check its tension at regular intervals, say about every 1,000 miles, and to retension the chain if necessary. Chain stretch depends, of course, to a considerable extent on whether or not the rider attends to its proper lubrication.

To check the tension of the secondary chain, first place the Bantam on its central stand (on spring-frame models the rear wheel *must* be in its *lowest* position). Then verify the chain whip (total up-and-down movement)

by applying pressure with the fingers to the bottom chain run about mid-way between the gear-box sprocket and the rear wheel sprocket. With the foot gear-change lever in neutral, turn over the rear wheel and verify the whip with the chain in a number of different positions. The whip with the chain in its tightest positon, should be ¾ in. (2 cm) on rigid frame models; ½ in. (1·27 cm) on Bantams with plunger springing; and ¾ in. on "swinging arm" models.

The adjustment of the secondary chain is effected by means of two draw-bolts (similar to those used on bicycles) in the rear-fork ends. Referring to Fig. 53, to re-tension the chain, slacken the rear-brake knurled adjuster-nut *C*, and both rear-wheel spindle nuts *A;* and then turn each adjuster nut *B* with a small spanner clockwise or anti-clockwise, as required, to tighten or slacken the chain respectively. When checking the tension after making an adjustment, be sure to push the wheel hard forward so that the spindle is hard up against the eyes of the draw-bolts. Be sure to tighten both adjuster nuts exactly the same amount so as to maintain the front and rear wheels in true alignment as described opposite. Having satisfied yourself that chain tension and wheel alignment are correct, firmly re-tighten both rear-wheel spindle nuts *A*.

Fitting the Spring Link. When replacing the old chain, or fitting a new one, always be extremely careful to fit the spring link so that its open end faces *away from* the direction of chain movement. Should a spring link come adrift when the chain is moving fast, a bad accident can be caused when the chain flies off the sprockets. Make absolutely sure that the spring link has not become distorted through careless removal, and that it beds down properly.

Checking Wheel Alignment. After removing the rear wheel and/or re-tensioning the secondary chain, it is advisable to check the alignment of the front and rear wheels in case the draw-bolt adjuster-nuts on each side of the rear wheel (*see* Fig. 53) have not been uniformly tightened. Misalignment of the wheels will cause uneven wear of the tyre treads, a tendency for skidding when the brakes are applied sharply, and imperfect steering when the hands are resting lightly on the handlebars.

To check that the alignment of the wheels is correct, set the front wheel so that it is pointing straight ahead, and then while standing at one end of the machine some distance away, glance along the line of the wheels. Any appreciable lack of alignment should at once be detected, assuming that you have good eyesight.

A more reliable and accurate method of checking the alignment, however, is to place a long straight-edge, the edge of a board, or a taut piece of string (tied to a peg in the ground at one end) so that it contacts the tyres of both wheels on one side of the Bantam. If the wheels are truly aligned, the straight-edge or string should contact simultaneously the front and rear walls of each tyre. But where a Bantam Competition model is

Fig. 53. The secondary chain and rear brake
adjustments

concerned, it is necessary to take into account the fact that the rear tyre is of
larger section than the front one.

If the wheels are found to be out of alignment, loosen the rear wheel-
spindle nuts and adjust the position of the rear wheel in the fork ends by
means of the draw-bolt adjuster-nuts shown at *B* in Fig. 53. Afterwards do
not forget to check that the chain tension is correct (*see* page 113) and that
the rear-wheel spindle-nuts *A* are firmly retightened.

To Remove the Front Wheel (Models D1, D3). Disconnect the brake
operating cable at the lever on the brake cover-plate and unscrew its adjuster
from the anchor-plate. Remove the two nuts from the wheel spindle. Next
undo the three mudguard-stay bolts on the near side and raise the near-side
fork leg sufficiently to enable the front wheel to drop out at an angle. It is
necessary to do this to avoid fouling by the fork anchor-plate on the brake
cover-plate.

To Remove Front Wheel (D5, D7, D7D/L). Disconnect the brake cable at
the lever on the brake cover-plate and unscrew its adjuster from the anchor
plate. Remove the nut which secures the cover-plate to the fork leg, and then
the two caps from the bottom of the fork legs. When doing this support the
front wheel. Then withdraw the wheel. Note that when the front wheel is
subsequently replaced the spindle ends must be level with the end faces of
the two caps.

To Remove Front Wheel (1968 (D14 Sports only) to 1970). Instructions for this operation are as those for models D7, except that the cover-plate carries a slotted arm which engages with a tongue on the fork leg. This avoids the use of a fixing nut.

To Remove the Rear Wheel. First disconnect the speedometer drive cable from the speedometer gearbox and remove the knurled adjuster nut from the rear-brake rod. Disconnect the secondary chain by removing its spring link, and unwinding the chain from the rear-wheel sprocket. It is best not to remove the chain from the gearbox sprocket. On Models D7, D10, D14, and Bantam 175 release the brake plate arm at the swinging arm. Afterwards loosen the rear-wheel spindle nuts sufficiently to enable the rear wheel to be withdrawn from the fork ends. During reassembly securely tighten the brake plate bolt at the swinging arm and check that the chain adjusters are firmly against the lug ends.

Replacing a Wheel. Be careful to locate the brake cover-plate anchorage properly, and make sure that it is secure. Before reconnecting the speedo-meter gearbox cable (rear wheel) first verify that the speedometer gearbox and cable casing are in proper alignment, because any sharp bends in the cable casing will probably result in a fracture of the cable itself.

Reconnect the front-brake cable or the rear-brake rod, the secondary chain (if dealing with a rear wheel), adjust the wheel spindle carefully in the fork ends, tighten the spindle lock-nuts securely (see that the chain adjusters abut the lugs), and finally check the brake adjustment (*see* page 111) for maximum efficiency.

Non-adjustable Wheel Bearings (Touring Models). The front and rear wheels on all Bantams have non-adjustable ball journal-bearing hubs. Provided that the ball bearings are greased regularly (*see* page 22), they should remain serviceable for the whole of the Bantam's operational life.

Gearbox Maintenance. On the Bantam the gearbox is, of course, in unit construction with the engine. Maintenance is confined to topping-up the gearbox and periodically changing the oil (*see* pages 18, 19).

In the unlikely event of some internal gearbox trouble developing, it is advisable for the average Bantam owner to entrust the dismantling, repair, and assembly of the gearbox to an authorized B.S.A. repair specialist.

Some Play in the Clutch Control is Essential. It is absolutely essential to the proper functioning of the clutch always to maintain a slight amount of play (say, $\frac{1}{32}$ in. to $\frac{1}{16}$ in.) in the clutch cable at the handlebar lever end, or in the clutch-operating mechanism (Fig. 55) comprising the slotted adjuster-pin (screwed into a quick-thread sleeve), the steel ball, and the clutch-operating rod (not shown in Fig. 55). Only by maintaining some play can

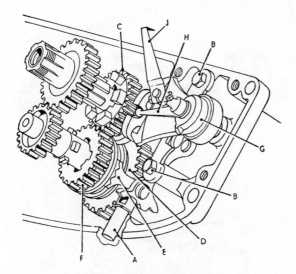

Fig. 54. The gear train in the B.S.A. three-speed gearbox

A. *Spring-loaded plunger*
B. *Bolts securing selector-mechanism*
C. *Mainshaft sliding gear*
D. *Layshaft first gear*
E. *Gear-selector arm*

F. *Layshaft second gear*
G. *Foot gear-change pedal shaft and spring-loaded claw assembly*
H. *Gear-position indicator lever*

you be sure that the clutch springs will exert full pressure on the plates and transmit the full power of the engine to the rear wheel.

Insufficient play causes a tendency for persistent clutch slip which is most irritating, and damaging to the friction inserts. Excessive play, on the other hand, while not being injurious to the friction-insert plates, renders gear changing somewhat uncertain and difficult. In either case an immediate adjustment is called for.

To Adjust the Clutch Control. Fig. 56 shows the very accessible external clutch adjustment on the near-side end of the gearbox mainshaft. The slotted adjuster-pin *C* is screwed into the clutch withdrawal quick-thread sleeve (*see* Fig. 55), and the lock nut *B* (Fig. 56) secures it firmly in position. The adjuster pin *C* presses against the long internal clutch-operating rod, and a steel ball is interposed between the pin and the rod.

Referring to Fig. 56 to adjust the clutch control, first slacken the lock-nut *B* with a suitable spanner. While holding the lock-nut, with a screwdriver turn the adjuster pin *C* *anti-clockwise* so that it is unscrewed one or two turns. Now, while still holding the lock-nut with a spanner, screw in the

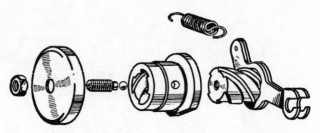

Fig. 55. Exploded view of clutch-operating mechanism

The long steel thrust-rod is not shown

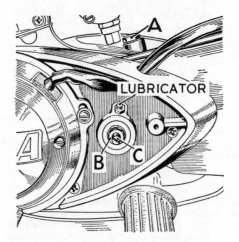

Fig. 56. The clutch-control adjustment on the near-side of the
power unit

adjuster pin gently until it is felt to meet resistance. Then unscrew the adjuster pin *half a turn* and, while preventing it from turning, retighten the lock-nut *B*. If the foregoing instructions are followed, the clutch control adjustment should be correct. But check the adjustment to make quite sure.

Dismantling the Bantam Clutch. To obtain access to the multiplate clutch it is, of course, necessary to remove the die-cast aluminium cover from the primary drive chain-case. Referring to Fig. 7, pull or tap the foot gear-change lever from its splined shaft after unscrewing and removing the pinch-bolt *C*. Also similarly remove the kick-starter lever from its shaft splines after taking out the pinch bolt *B*. Next unscrew the five cheese-headed screws *D*. To ensure correct replacement of the screws, note that there are three screws at the rear, and two *longer* ones at the *front* of the chain-case cover. If it is stiff, tap it gently with a mallet, but make no attempt to prise it off. Examine the compressed-paper washer fitted between the cover and case. If this is in any way damaged, it must be renewed.

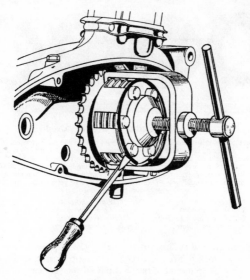

Fig. 57. Removing the steel circlip before dismantling the B.S.A. clutch

The springs have been compressed with the B.S.A. service tool and the circlip is shown partly prised out with a screwdriver

Removal of the primary chain-case cover exposes to view (*see* Fig. 52) the entire clutch assembly, the engine sprocket, the non-adjustable primary chain, the kick-starter quadrant, and the clock-type return spring for the kick-starter.

Should it be desired to dismantle the clutch plate assembly in order to have some new inserts fitted, first remove the primary chain by releasing the spring link. On 1950–70 models remove the steel cover-plate (the outer one) held by three set-screws to the spring-cup plate. Now fit the B.S.A. service tool No. 61–3191 over the clutch assembly in the manner illustrated in Fig. 57 and slowly turn the tommy-bar until the six helical compression

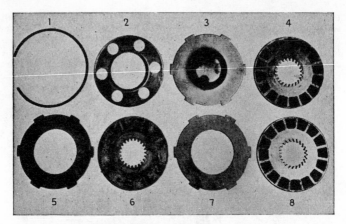

Fig. 58. The clutch plates removed

The correct reassembly order is 8–2. Plate (8) goes next to the plain sprocket plate (not shown). The six spring cups (also not shown) fit into the holes in plate (2), and the inner ends of the springs press against the outside of the pressure plate (3) the dished inside of which contacts the mushroom head of the clutch-operating thrust rod. On 1950–7 models a cover plate is fitted outside the retaining circlip and is secured by three set-screws. On the 1958–66 Models D5, D7 and D7D/L the clutch has three solid friction-plates bonded with Neolangite segments

1. Steel circlip
2. Spring-cup plate
3. Pressure plate (dished)
4. Cork-insert plate
5. Plain steel-plate
6. Cork-insert plate
7. Plain steel-plate
8. Cork-insert plate

springs are compressed sufficiently to enable you to prise off with a screw-driver, as shown in Fig. 57, the large steel circlip shown at (1) in Fig. 58. Referring to Fig. 58, removal of the circlip (and the service tool) permits of the spring-cup plate (2), the six spring cups (not shown), the six helical springs (not shown), the pressure plate (3), and the plain steel and friction-insert (later models friction pads) plates (4)–(8) being withdrawn for inspection in this order from the clutch body. For 1967–70 models, an additional friction-pad plate is fitted, increasing the quantity of these plates to four, with a corresponding increase in the width of the clutch. Also remove the mushroom-headed steel thrust rod from the drilled main-shaft.

For the purpose of fitting new inserts to the clutch plates, it is not necessary to remove the clutch sprocket-plate (which has no inserts), nor the clutch hub from the splined mainshaft. The reassembly of the clutch plates should be effected in the reverse order of dismantling.

Fit alternately the plain steel-plates, friction insert/pad plates. The correct assembly order is shown in Fig. 58 for the three friction-plate clutches. There will, or course, be an extra one of each of the plain and friction plates on models for 1967–70. Do not forget to replace the mushroom-headed steel thrust-rod before the pressure plate is replaced. Oil the rod before inserting it. To replace the steel circlip, you must first compress the six helical springs with the service tool as shown in Fig. 57. See that the circlip beds home snugly into the groove provided. On 1950–70 Bantams replace the outer cover and secure it to the spring-cup plate by means of the three set-screws.

When reconnecting the non-adjustable primary chain, make sure that its spring link is fitted with the closed end facing the direction of chain movement. After replacing the primary drive chain-case cover and compressed-paper washer (grease it on both sides), fit the kick-starter and the foot gear-change levers, and see that their pinch-bolts are firmly retightened.

Plunger Suspension Units (Models D1, D3). If as the result of an accident involving damage to the units, or in the very unlikely event of excessive

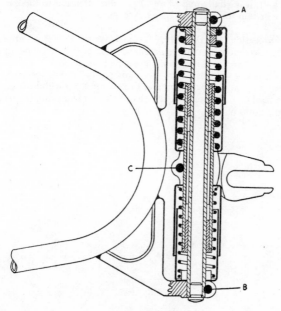

Fig. 59. Sectional view showing details of plunger suspension unit
(Models D1, D3)

Pinch-bolts are fitted at A, B, and C

plunger movement (*see* page 108) occurring, it is necessary to dismantle each rear-suspension unit; do this as described below.

First remove the rear wheel (*see* page 116) and also the silencer. To remove the silencer, slacken the nut on the clip securing the silencer to the exhaust pipe, and remove the nut on the pinch-bolt *B* (Fig. 59) securing the silencer lug to the off-side rear-suspension unit.

Referring to Fig. 59, remove the pinch-bolts *A* and *B*. Next tap out the central column of each rear-suspension unit from below, and withdraw the column through the top lug. Having done this, slide off sideways from the bottom lug the remaining components of each suspension unit. Lay them on a clean sheet of paper ready for complete stripping-down. Note the relative and exact positions of the various components to ensure correct reassembly.

To separate the spring plunger (comprising the wheel-spindle bracket and attached bearing sleeve) from the bearing sleeve, it is only necessary to tap out the pinch-bolt *C*. Observe that this pinch-bolt engages a notch in the bearing sleeve, and that the pinch bolts at *A* and *B* similarly engage in notches in the central column (removed). When reassembling each sus-pension unit, it is vitally important to pay due attention to these notches and to be certain that they are correctly aligned.

Rear Suspension (D5, D7, D10, D14, and Bantam 175). Both suspension units are sealed and require no maintenance whatever. The "swinging arm" pivot, however, requires occasional greasing (*see* page 24).

Should the rear suspension units be damaged or become inefficient after a very big mileage, remove them and fit new ones. To withdraw the units from the Bantam frame, remove the pivot bolts at the top and the retaining nuts at the bottom.

Index